GROW
with your plants
The Mother Earth Hassle-Free Way
by Lynn & Joel Rapp

GROW
with your plants
The Mother Earth Hassle-Free Way
by Lynn & Joel Rapp

Published by J. P. Tarcher, Inc., Los Angeles

Distributed by Hawthorn Books, Inc., New York

For some reason, it is considered an honor to have a book dedicated to you.

We can well see the logic if the book is a critical and commercial success.

We can also see the logic even if it's not.

But the truth is, it's more fulfilling if the book is a hit.

So—we hope that this dedication is a *complete* honor for the man to whom it's made.

Perhaps if you knew Philip Rapp—"Grampa" Earth, we call him—you'd know why he deserves more than a thousand dedications on a thousand hits.

Library of Congress Catalog Card Number: 74-79509
ISBN: 0-87477-029-7 (softcover)
      0-87477-030-0 (hardcover)

Manufactured in the United States of America

Published by J. P. Tarcher, Inc.
9110 Sunset Blvd., Los Angeles, Calif. 90069

Published simultaneously in Canada by
Prentice-Hall of Canada, Ltd.
1870 Birchmount Road, Scarborough, Ontario

1 2 3 4 5 6 7 8 9 0

Table of Contents

Thanks for allowing us to spread the green word.

Foreword

Here we go again, Philodendron Phans!

For the uninitiated, our first book was called *Mother Earth's Hassle-Free Indoor Plant Book,* and to the initiated, we say—THANKS!

Thanks for making our first book a success beyond our wildest dreams—dreams we had because we want EVERYBODY to get involved with houseplants; thanks for making it possible for us to share with you the incredible joys of the "houseplant experience" and allowing us to Spread the Good Green Word.

Thanks, too, for all the laughs and joy you've given us over the phone and in your letters about your favorite plants and growing experiences: We will never forget the lady in Chicago who tried to determine if a yellowing condition in her Schefflera was an iron-deficiency known as chlorosis, or just plain overwatering—and when she discovered her tree was sick as a result of both lack of iron and too much to drink, she diagnosed its condition as "Chlorosis of the Leafer." Or the gentleman in San Francisco who had tried everything in the horticultural world to save his favorite Fern from a premature trip to that Great Greenhouse in the Sky, and finally, in total desperation, claims to have given it mouth-to-leaf resuscitation. And of course that very charming lady in Philadelphia who, after twelve years of failure, sadly decided that the only place for her orchid plant was on her daughter's prom dress.

We honestly believe that in Book #1 we said just about every basic thing you need to know with regard to what you can do for your plants. This time we have another goal. We're going to try and help you discover what your plants can do for you!

Before we start, it might be worthwhile to fill in a few gaps on what's happened to the houseplant business—or, more importantly, to people's attitudes about houseplants since the advent of what we call The Great Green Rush some four years ago.

In the year 1974 we are undergoing what has been popularly described as an Energy Crisis. It means that because of a somewhat critical fuel shortage, we've had to drive a great deal less than before, we've had to keep our thermostats set at 68 degrees instead of 74, we've had to start riding bicycles and are rediscovering a long lost art called "walking," and because of food shortages we've had to cut down on the amount of meat we eat and start being more conscious of not only our total intake but of things we can grow and cook ourselves—lots of little inconveniences that may eventually be the salvation of us all. Including our houseplants.

You see, from a purely physical point of view, houseplants prefer the cooler temperatures we're now forced to keep in our homes, and from a psychological point of view, they're benefiting because at long last people are not just buying houseplants for beauty and decor—they NEED them for the joy of having an open honest communication with a lot of honest, open, innocent, alive, little green things.

The houseplants can feel it. Thus they thrive. Thus their owners have the courage to buy more plants. Thus there is The Great Green Rush. And thus the houseplant industry has grown over 400 percent in a scant four years. So because of the great interest in plants that has developed since people are being forced to stay inside more, and because most urban centers are sadly lacking in significant greenery, and because plants are cheaper to buy and care for than any other kind of housepets. . . . Because of all these things—office planners are using plants (the hardies that grow well under fluorescent lights) as dividers instead of the old depressing plywood slabs. Plants are now an integral part of bank, restaurant, in fact, practically all business decor, and plants have become a natural part of the inventory of antique stores, shoe stores, picture-framing stores, supermarkets, discount stores, etc. The Great Green Rush is not a fad—it's a fact—indeed it can become a factor in our lives if we are only wise enough to let it.

So we'll try to do what the title says: Help you grow with your plants; impart to you, from our own experience and the experiences we've heard from thousands of you all over the country, little things that can make your houseplants a source of constant extra joy. We'll even throw in a chapter now and then that won't be of the most practical use (the chapter on medicinal herbs, for instance), but that will, we hope, provide you with some interesting information and more understanding of just how important plants can be to us all. We'll try to make you see the importance of Turning-On-A-Friend—man, woman, child, whomever. We'll give you some information in areas we didn't deal with the first time around. And, most of all, we'll hope you come to derive as much fun from living in Green-Land as we have.

Thanks for bearing with us through this preamble, so now:

Let's get growing!

As an "offshoot" of The Great Green Rush, there are by actual count 3,841 books on the market that deal with the subject of indoor plants.

Of that number, 1,885 are devoted entirely to plant consciousness, i.e., is it good to talk to your plants, can plants feel, should you play music to your plants, did a band of dastardly Dieffenbachias actually plan and commit the infamous Brink's robbery, etc.

The above paragraphs are a blatant lie, of course, but in a book of this kind, a semiscientific-type effort, it's important to quote figures.

The fact is, we really don't know exactly how many books there are on plants or how many of them really get into plant consciousness. We do know one thing, however—

This is another one.

By this time, most people who really care at all about the subject have concluded that to take a totally negative position is not only *dumb,* it's probably dangerous. People who are willing to stand up and say flatly that plants don't have feelings might just as well knock Motherhood or Mickey Mouse. There is entirely too much scientific evidence to prove that plants, in fact, *do* have feelings, the extent of which is the source of a constant and continuing probe.

There is an outstanding book on the subject by Peter Tompkins and Christopher Bird called *The Secret Life of Plants,* so for us to take too much time to discuss it would be unnecessary and besides, there's a paper shortage.

Neither of us has ever hooked a polygraph to a Polypodium to find out if it loves or hates its neighbors; we've never gone into a lab and fiddled with a Fiddle-Leaf Fig or its pot-mate. We are, as we said in our first book, neither botanists nor horticulturists, and we certainly aren't parapsychologists. We're just two ordinary people having an extraordinary love affair with plants.

We talk to them, we play music for them, and we *know* they appreciate it.

In our travels, we're not only being constantly asked our opinion on this subject, but we've come across some stories that we know you won't find in any of those 1,885 aforementioned books. These stories have been told to us

Chapter 1.
Plant Lore

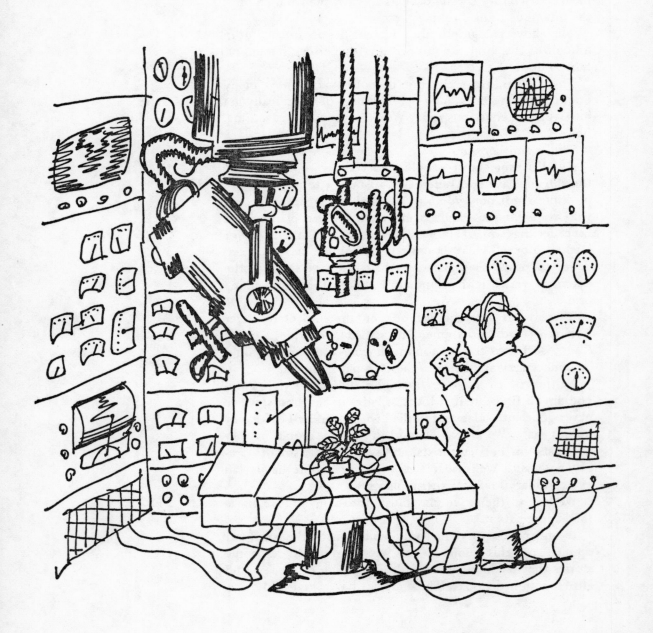

by other ordinary people involved with plants—people whose closest brush with scientific experiment was the formaldehyde-covered earthworm they were forced to face in High School Biology II.

But they're true. We know it because plant people don't lie (a glittering generality), and besides, a couple of these stories happened to us.

For instance:

In our living room there are close to three hundred plants. Since we're off to work before 9 o'clock in the morning and rarely return home until well after 6, it has been our habit to leave the radio on for the plants while we're gone.

Not long ago we left for a two-week lecture tour. Naturally we made arrangements for our Mother Earth Plant Service to make twice-weekly visits to our house to mist, water, clip and feed. But when we got home from the trip, somehow the plants just didn't look right. We were absolutely certain that our service hadn't goofed because (a) they were taking care of the bosses' house, and (b) they had charged us a bloody fortune. Lynn decided she'd check them all, and I headed for the bedroom.

It was a Sunday afternoon, so I decided to watch a sporting event on TV. As I lay comfortably back, secure in the knowledge that Lynn was busily reintroducing herself to all the plants, my serenity was interrupted by Ms. Mother Earth coming into the room.

"I don't know what it is, but something's wrong," she said.

"You're telling me?" I replied. "The Rams just fumbled on New York's 20, Jack Nicklaus four-putted a green, and Wide World of Sports is only showing fifteen different events instead of twenty. Oh, the pain. . . ."

"I meant with the plants," she replied testily. "Everything's been properly cared for, but—well, they all look a little off—sort of droopy."

I got up and went into the living room, and as we walked around and looked at the plants I had to agree. They *were* off. Maybe a stranger wouldn't have noticed, but believe me, to the practiced eye of the parents, the children were definitely not up to snuff.

I shook my head helplessly. "No mealybug. No sign of

red spider. Nobody seems to be too wet or too dry."

"Wait a minute," said Lynn, a look of discovery beginning to appear on her face. "Do you hear that?"

I listened for a minute. "I don't hear anything."

"Exactly," she beamed. "The radio's off!" She turned the radio on, left the room for about three minutes and then came back, smiling triumphantly.

"I just talked to the plant service," she said, "and they told me the day after we left they came over to tend the plants and thought they should turn off the radio. The Energy Crisis and all. Do you realize these plants have been in this room without music for over two weeks?"

By now the strains of "Tie a Yellow Ribbon 'round the Old Oak Tree" were wafting from the stereo.

I wondered. Could it possibly be? Could even I dare to believe it?

The next day those plants were back in A-1 shape again. Perfect. No more sagging, drooping, or curling.

I finally dared to believe it.

We believe this one, too. Robert L. Green is a tremendously charming man who is not only fashion director for *Playboy* Magazine but whose thumb completely matches his name.

Robert L. has a farm in Bucks County, Pennsylvania. It's absolutely beautiful—65 acres with a house built in 1730-something by an honest-to-God relative of William Penn. And where there isn't wheat growing, there are huge beds for flowering plants. To give you an idea just how huge, every year Robert L. plants over a thousand Tulip and Lily bulbs in those beds—with a little help from his friends, of course—and then in April, when all the flowers are in magnificent full bloom, he hosts a tremendous party, the guest list of which contains lots of friends and also lots and lots of important business connections.

You know what we mean. To Robert L.—just like it would be to you—it's a Very Important Party, and it simply cannot be a success without the eye-boggling panorama of rich green fields and brilliantly colored Tulips and perfect, creamy-white Lilies.

Every year things had gone perfectly: The bulbs had been planted in November, the plants had begun to sprout

Every year he hosts a tremendous party.

"... Today the stock market was down again, prices were up again, and several smog alerts...."

and appear by the beginning of February and by April—
Voilá!—a miracle of color.

Suddenly, a couple of years ago, it's almost the end of
March, the foliage of the Tulips and Lilies is all standing
tall and erect—but, Oh, God, no don't let this happen—so
far no sign of a bud. Not even the *beginning* indications of
Plant Parenthood.

Robert L., a man not easily given to alarm, did *not*
become alarmed as five days before the party there were
still no blooms.

No, indeed.

He simply panicked.

He marched outside, stood furiously over each bed of
plants and shouted: "Listen, you little bitches; in five days
two hundred people will be here for food and you. I'm
already cooking pies and turkeys, and you—you just sit
there and do nothing! I won't have it, do you hear me??
This party means everything to me, it's got to be perfect,
and besides it's costing me a fortune!" Robert L. raised his
fist in the air: "I have only one thing to say: Bloom, damn
you, bloom!"

The next day—and it's the truth, believe us—the plants
had begun to bloom. The day after, they were about
halfway home, and when the first guests arrived for the
party, they were literally dazzled by the sight of thousands
of incredibly beautiful Tulips and Lilies, blooming like
mad all over the farm.

Our most far-out story probably comes from a student
of botany we know at a highly reputable college in
California.

This somewhat skeptical scientist friend decided to try
an experiment with plants: He would put three sets of the
hardiest plants—Sansevieria, Chinese Evergreens, Nephthytis, and the like—in three separate rooms under identical growing conditions.

In the first room, he played only classical music to the
plants, and the plants thrived.

In the second room, he played only rock music—and
those plants thrived.

In the third room, he played only the news.

And those plants died.

We leave it to you to draw your own conclusions.

Onward. ☙

Peperomia

wandering Jew

Spider plant

Asparagus fern

Coleus

creeping Charlie

Bird's Nest Fern

Purple Velvet

Cactus

Succulents

The Almost Hassle-Free Plants

Let's face it, we're all frustrated as hell. Frustrated by the irrefutable fact our brains are simply bursting with profound thoughts, easy explanations of heretofore insoluble problems, never-before-spoken philosophies on marriage and child-raising, "The Foolproof Way to Inner Peace"—and, of course, there isn't one among us who couldn't run things better than *they* do. Right?

Come on, admit it. You're just like the rest of us—aching to scream out how YOU feel about things and Please God won't somebody listen?

Ah, but how do you get the chance? Is there a forum where any of us plain ordinary people can speak out and actually have other plain ordinary people listen and respond?

You bet there is! It's called The Two-Way Radio Talk Show, and of all the marvelous things that have happened to us as a result of our "plant trip," the opportunity to hear from you about your plant problems (and your general philosophies as well) is right at the top of the list.

It's amazing how easily plant-talk can turn into plain-talk. We don't know why, but so many times we found ourselves listening to your feelings about how your life-style has changed since you became involved with plants; or how your marriage has improved since you and your mate (and even your children) have discovered the family that "sprays together stays together" or that "pots together does lots together" or that _____ (fill in your own witticism here and send it to us for the second printing). We even found ourselves engaging with you in dialogue on the ever-interesting and always different subject of child-raising, usually brought up as a comparison to raising a plant from budhood through adolescence.

The main topic, however, is Plants, Plants and More Plants, and as a result of all the green gossip we have accrued we have come to several conclusions, not least among them the conviction that the Fifteen Guaranteed-to-Grow plants we talked about in our first book might just *not* be the only Hassle-Free Plants there are. That list consisted of Aspidistra, Boston Fern, Chinese Evergreens, Dieffenbachia, Dracaenas, Ficus, Grape Ivy, Maranta, Nephthytis, Palms, Philodendrons, Piggyback, Pothos, Sansevieria and Spathiphyllum. Each of these plants is available all over the country, and comes in an almost infinite

Chapter 2.
More
Hassle-Free Plants
(Well, Almost)

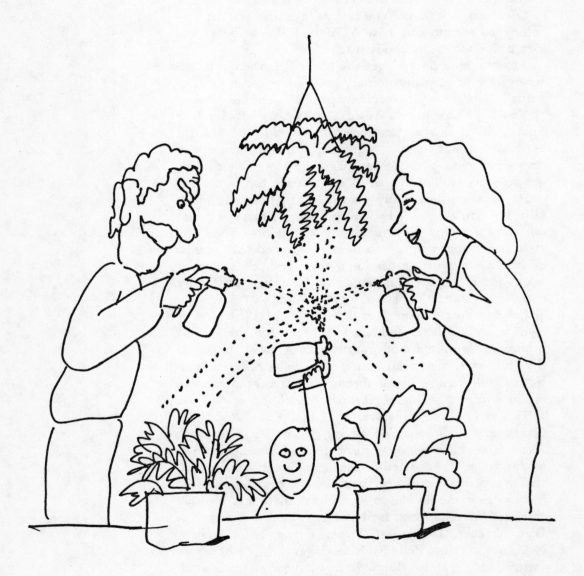

The family that sprays together stays together.

variety of shapes, sizes, variegations, etc., so if you choose from the fifteen you can actually have over a hundred plants without any two looking alike. That ought to be enough for anyone but Luther Burbank. It ought to be, but it isn't, and now, through the help of our friends, we've discovered that certain other plants are Hassle-Free (well, Almost) and also available just about everywhere. Since many of our friends have had extraordinary luck with these plants, we thought we'd mention them, with a small admonition:

If you purchase one of the plants we are about to discuss, do not expect to get a 90-day or 5,000-root leaf replacement warranty. (In fact, if you purchase any of the fifteen above-named Hassle-Free Plants don't expect a warranty, either.) But don't be afraid to take a plant back where you bought it if it appears to have the vapors. Almost all reputable nurseries will be glad to help you diagnose your plant problems, not only because they care about seeing their plants happy, but because they want to see their customers happy, too.

Okay, so here they are. Remember, even though these plants are not quite as Hassle-Free and thus require spending more time and effort to get good results, the rewards are greater also. The personal involvement leads to personal growth. You'll find yourself gaining more patience and a greater sense of responsibility. And you'll feel good about yourself, which ain't bad!

This is probably as good a place as any to mention something we feel is vital in making your Plant-Care as Hassle-Free and beneficial to your plants as possible.

That something is: BE ORGANIZED.

We are not, by nature, organized people, and we really envy those friends of ours who always know immediately where the insurance policies are or can pull the right receipt out of the right drawer at any given moment's notice. But since we now have over four hundred plants that depend on us for their watering and misting and trimming and bathing and feeding, we've found we simply *have* to keep a calendar to know exactly when they've been fed last and when they're due to be fed again. (As you probably already know, overwatering and overfeeding do in more plants than neglect.)

Be organized.

To make the entire process simpler, we keep all our supplies in a large picnic basket: food, vitamins, scissors, spray bottle, towel, fork (for "tilling" hard soil to allow air to get to the roots), sponge and toothbrush and "bubble bath" (a mild biodegradable dishwashing liquid) to keep our plants clean, and whatever else we've added for our particular plant needs. Everything is together so that we don't have to spend an extra half-hour trying to find everything. We suggest you do the same. It really does make keeping up your Plantation a lot easier.

Another bit of advice from Mother Earth. Most plants have a stick in their soil when you buy them, giving their Latin name, their common name and sometimes even instructions about how to care for them. If they don't, ask your nurseryperson to give you these details and make your own stick. It'll help you learn their names, and that's important.

While you're at it, why not do what we do? After their Latin Names and their common names, add their Christian names . . . you know, Sam, Kevin, Becky. . . .

Now that we've gone over the basic ground rules, let's check our program for the names and care of our Almost Hassle-Free Plant Team.

Peperomia—No, this is not related to the Pepper family (only one P, notice?). It's simply a lovely houseplant that comes in dozens of varieties, the most common being the Watermelon, which you can recognize by its broad oval leaves that bear markings almost identical to the markings of a watermelon (but with the advantage of no seeds). Emerald Ripple has a dark green wrinkled-looking leaf (very similar to your green thumb after it's been immersed too long in hot water). The Variegated or Obtusifolia is a beautiful plant with thick green and yellow leaves.

All Peperomias need essentially the same care. Give them good indirect light (they will simply wilt and let go in a dim situation), and most importantly, keep them on the dry side—too much water, they get soggy stems—too little, they become brittle and break.

They should be misted lightly once a week to keep their leaves clean, but they do not like a daily bath. Don't be alarmed if an occasional stem gets droopy and then can be

23

pulled out of the pot almost as if it had no connection. It happens. But if it happens too often, you're overwatering.

Go ahead. Try a Peperomia. You'll probably do pretty well. But a word of caution: Don't try adding it to your pizza. For that you have to grow a peperoni.

Spider Plant, or Chlorophytum—This one is sometimes called Airplane Plant (in the case of ours, it's called Stanley) and is distinguished by its bushy white and green thin-leafed crown and its trailing, cream-colored stems at the end of which are its "babies," little tufts of white and green that are, indeed, babies. As soon as they form large enough roots you may cut that creamy "umbilical cord" and pot up your new Spider Plants. (See Chapter 6 on Propagation.)

Where should they be kept? In a good, light place, very near a window but as with all other plants, not resting directly against the glass. As a generality, Spider Plants do better outside than in, but kept in proper light and watered when dryish, they *can* live inside. One caution: It is a characteristic of the Spider Plant to turn yellow or brown at the tips of its leaves. This could be caused by not enough light or even overwatering, but generally speaking, when it comes to the Spider, brown tips are simply the nature of the beast. The remedy? A bit more humidity will perhaps delay the browning, but in the long run, every Spider Plant needs a good, careful haircut (trim the brown tips with your scissors) at least once a month.

So get yourself a Spider Plant. Just remember who it was who lured the fly into its parlor.

Coleus—Ahhh, there aren't many houseplants that can match the Coleus for sheer vibrant excitement. That's part of the reason we listed it as a Glamour Plant in our first book, along with such plants as Croton, Maidenhair Fern, Zebra Plant, etc., which are always the ones that neophyte plant-buyers "simply *must* have," but because of their relative difficulty to cultivate indoors simply shouldn't have or at least shouldn't have to start with.

However, because many of you have told us your Coleus is thriving, we have decided to promote this brilliantly colored beauty from Glamour Plant to Almost Hassle-Free.

Seen mostly in shades of deep purple or purple and green, Coleus is essentially an outdoor bedding plant for spring and summer seasons, but is often raised in greenhouses and then successfully transferred indoors.

A bushy plant best suited for hanging or placing on a stand, Coleus should be kept in a light, cool place, watered frequently (it'll wilt quickly if not kept moist) and fed a little more than your average houseplant (twice per month during the growth period rather than once).

Growth Period

Why, you might ask, would a plant not grow all year long inside where it is not subject to seasonal changes? Because, we would answer, there are seasons in your house just as there are outdoors.

We doubt you'll have much rain in your living room or that you'll want to spread a picnic blanket in the dining room during the summer, but obviously unless you are growing your plants under artificial light there will be less light in winter than in spring and summer; and heat and humidity factors will vary according to the seasons indoors as well. Therefore, consider your indoor plants' growth period to be similar to that of their outdoor brothers and sisters—spring and summer. If some of them seem to stop growing altogether during the winter months, just understand that they have gone to the plant equivalent of Miami Beach and will return to begin growing anew come March or early April.

The main problem people seem to have with Colei—other than not keeping them in enough light—is allowing them to get leggy, letting their long graceful stems begin to trail, sapping the roots' strength so that the crown is virtually devoid of foliage. If this happens, the plant must be cut back, using scissors and cutting the stems off so that they are only 4 to 6 inches long. This may pain you, but keep in mind it is the best thing for the plant and be heartened by the fact you can make new Coleus plants with the cuttings. (See Chapter 6 on Propagation.)

To avoid the problem in the first place, practice some preventive medicine by *pinching back* new growth as it appears on the runners—a simple operation which consists of removing new growth with thumb and forefinger (making a little scissors with your nails), to ensure that the plant will develop into a full, lush healthy specimen. This principle works on every plant and is the only way to prevent premature baldness, which is important since making a plant toupee can be a hairy situation.

With Coleus, keep a sharp eye out for mealybug, that dreaded white-fuzzy-cottony-looking Plant Killer. For some reason, mealybugs are especially attracted to Coleus, perhaps because, as we said, Coleus is so irresistibly attractive. If you can't get rid of the mealybug in time by attacking the little critters directly with a Q-tip dipped in alcohol or spraying with a mild houseplant insecticide, you'll simply have to cut the whole plant back, and as they say in certain sporting circles, wait till next year.

But if you can find a nice light place to keep it while it's recuperating, remembering to water and pinch back during the rather lengthy convalescence, it's worth the wait.

A very effective way to keep your coleus supremely happy (and this goes for other hanging plants as well—Ferns, Grape Ivy, Spider Plants, etc.) is to plant it in a bare-root basket.

Bare-Root Basket

"What's that?" asked our friend Madeline, who typed this manuscript, as her Selectric sat humming on the desk waiting to clack out the answer:

"A bare-root basket is a bowl-shaped aluminum wire thing that is available in almost any nursery or plant shop in varying sizes from as small as 4 or 5 inches in diameter all the way up to 16 or 18 inches."

"Doesn't the dirt fall out?" Madeline asked, beginning to become a bit pesty in light of the fact she gets paid by the minute.

But her question is valid and so we hope is our answer: You keep the dirt from falling out by lining your bare-root basket (see above) with sphagnum moss which has been soaked with water and then squeezed out—and before she opens her mouth again—sphagnum moss is a greenish-brown mossy substance that grows wild in parts of Canada but is domesticated and bagged for sale at your local nursery or plant shop.

Once you have lined your basket with a layer of moss firmly packed down and at least 3 inches thick, keeping in mind that the moss becomes the pot *and* the planting medium, remove your plant from its original container, gently take off as much soil from the roots as you can, and

Mealybugs are particularly attracted to Coleus.

then plop it into its new moss-covered cottage. Add just enough sterilized indoor potting mix (available at nurseries everywhere) to hold it in place, and fill up the rest of the basket with more sphagnum moss, also making sure that the moss is firmly packed. Water thoroughly and then hang your newly bare-rooted basket in a spot where it can drip freely until it's ready to hang up in its permanent home.

No, Madeline, it is not more hassle to water your bare-root basket because most hanging plants are housed in containers with holes in the bottom just like that Kangaroo Vine that's dangling precariously over your head, so you'll have to take *them* to the sink or outside in the shade to water them, too.

"Can't you just put a bucket under them and water them where they hang?"

"Yes, Madeline, you can do that if you wish."

Now we trust there will be no further silly questions.

Creeping Charlie—A light green, waxy-leafed plant that grows a gorgeous bushy crown and long, lush trailers. If it's happy.

This popular plant needs very good light; water thoroughly when dryish, feed once a month, pinch back frequently, and mist only about once a week. (They have succulent-like leaves which tend to wrinkle up if misted too frequently.)

We've seen them looking great in the house, but the very best specimens of this plant are always the ones that have been grown outdoors.

So if you see your Charlie creeping toward the front door, don't stand in his way.

Everybody's entitled to a better life, right?

Purple Velvet—If ever a plant looked exactly like its name, the Purple Velvet, or Gynura, is that plant, sure enough.

We suppose it's redundant to say it, but the Purple Velvet, another vining beauty, is a rich purple color with velvety looking leaves.

Its care is the same as for the Coleus—good, indirect light, keep moist at all times, pinch back frequently and beware of mealybugs. (Isn't it odd that a regal plant like the Purple Velvet should contract as common a disease as mealybug, rather than one of the Royal Diseases like gout or catarrh?)

28

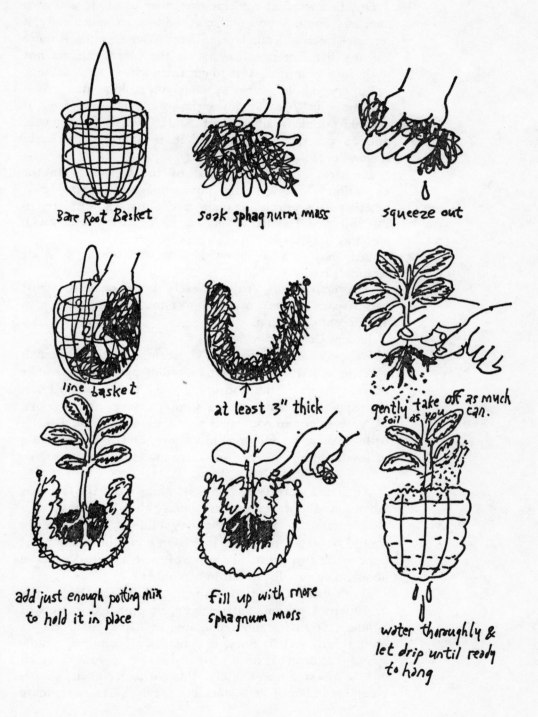

Bare Root Basket

soak sphagnum moss

squeeze out

line basket

at least 3" thick

gently take off as much soil as you can.

add just enough potting mix to hold it in place

fill up with more sphagnum moss

water thoroughly & let drip until ready to hang

One last word about this particular plant. If you own one, and one day you notice an odd—more specifically, a terrible—smell in your house, check your Gynura. If there are any little orange flowers on the plant, run, do not walk, for a pair of scissors to cut them off.

But try to hold your nose while you're doing it.

Wandering Jew—Tradescantia, or Wandering Jew, is another popular trailing plant. And as well as growing wild outside practically anywhere, it is almost completely Hassle-Free as an indoor plant.

Its care is much like that of the Coleus, with the exception of the watering. Your average Wandering Jew—whether it be purple, or plain green, or the almost irresistible silver and white variety—doesn't like quite as much water as the Coleus.

But maybe a little chicken soup once in a while wouldn't hurt.

Asparagus Fern—Virtually every book on houseplants lists Asparagus Fern as an almost mandatory addition to any decent collection.

Except this one.

We will admit that we've seen lots of Asparagus sprengeri—that's a rich green, cascading plant with pine-like needles on its fronds and upon which occasional red berries appear at least once a year—do very well indoors. We've even got an Asparagus plumosus, a feathery, delicate little beauty, in our breakfast room, and it hasn't had a yellow needle in weeks. But these are exceptions, not the rule.

Asparagus Fern (which gets its name from the fact that when new shoots appear, just before they open they very closely resemble the common vegetable Asparagus) really should be in a spot where it gets an enormous amount of light, since this plant, like some of the others we've talked about, is essentially an outdoor number.

Don't water too often. Better repot frequently as it has a giant root system. Furthermore, be prepared for lots of bending, stooping and vacuuming as Asparagus Fern, no matter how well it does, is constantly producing yellow spines that drop off onto your floor—or into your Granola.

Bird's-Nest Fern—Frankly, this particular plant, a spectacular member of the Asplenium family, was a last-minute

*If you notice
an odd smell,
check your Gynura.*

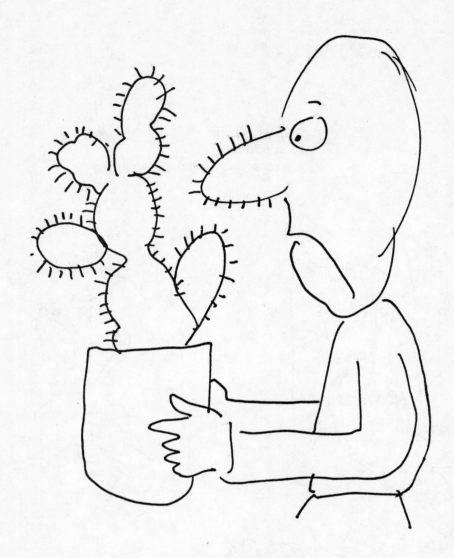

How to take care of cactus?
Carefully!

entry into the Almost Hassle-Free Sweepstakes. It probably would never have made the field if we hadn't been at a friend's house recently and noticed a beautiful specimen thriving near a dining room window and discovered, to our joyful surprise, it was the same plant he'd bought at our shop almost three years before.

It really is a showy plant, this Bird's-Nest, even though you'll rarely find a bird nesting in its pot. Its undivided fronds grow upward from a center crown and are a shiny apple-green. It's fun to watch a new frond begin to unfurl from this center, and although the plant grows slowly indoors (outdoors in the shade—look out for nest-hunting Eagles!), its fronds can reach 5 feet in height and it can have a 10- to 12-inch frondspread if placed in good filtered light and kept slightly damp, not thoroughly watered like its Boston and Maidenhair Fern cousins.

On a healthy plant, a young frond will always be poking up its little head, provided you feed sparingly twice a month, keep the plant cool and mist it daily to help minimize dry, brown edges.

The plant also·has a tendency to develop brown "blemishes" in the middle of its fronds, but this is perfectly natural and must be accepted just as you easily accept a freckle or two on your human companions.

Cacti and Succulents—We touched on Cacti in our first book, and since our fingers were bleeding for weeks, we thought we'd leave well enough alone this time.

But let's face it, Cacti and Succulents are indeed Almost Hassle-Free—the only hassle being you must have a very, very bright spot in your home in order for a member of this family to thrive—in fact, almost direct sunlight. So it would be fitting to expand just a bit more on what we admit is a rather dry subject. Or a thorny problem. Or—okay we'll stop punning on Cacti if you'll stop needling us.

Anyway, Cacti are native to every state in the Union except Maine, New Hampshire, and Vermont, and since you folks in those states can grow Popsicles it all works out in the end.

Some of the most popular forms of Cactus are—and please bear with us on these scientific names—Cephalocereus senilis (Old Man), an upright little number that has a bushy white head of hair; Pachycereus marginatus (Organ Pipe), prized for its clean, fast growth; Oseocereus (are *you* serious?); Celsianus, noted for its soft, silky hair; Echino-cactus grusonii (Golden Ball), known for its golden spines; and Pereskia, the Parent of all Cacti, a full-time job in itself.

How to take care of your Cacti?

Carefully.

And just remember some simple basics: Almost all Cacti are about 90 percent water and require a sandy, porous soil that will drain off surplus moisture quickly without drying out too rapidly. Cacti require feeding, as their natural desert soil is rich in lime and decomposed leaf-mold, so about once every two or three months you should give them a feeding of a low-nitrogen plant food, following the directions on the bottle you buy. Cacti like to be sprayed lightly on especially hot days, but never with cold water. When grown indoors, they'll live nicely in those "too bright" areas where other plants burn. Our Cacti and Succulents are doing extremely well under regular light, which is on eight hours a day. Fluorescent light is terrific for them, too.

Succulents, which are related to the Cactus family, do not have spines or needles. Their leaves are usually fat, shiny and smooth, except for an occasional fancy dresser like the Panda plant, whose soft, fuzzy foliage feels much like a suede coat. There are thousands of different varieties, and though you will need a very bright spot for your Succulents, we think you'll find them fascinating and fun.

The leaves of a Succulent are full of moisture and the root system is generally quite simple, so they don't require much water. Let the plant get very dry and then give it a thorough watering. A container without a drainage hole is a no-no, and these little cuties don't want to be misted every day. In fact, they can go weeks without so much as a shower. (We have a third cousin who thinks he's a Succulent, but that's another story. . . .)

Succulents don't eat much, either, although some are rather chubby like the readily available Crassula (Jade) family and the not-so-available but really incredible Baby Toes. (These fat little numbers, which resemble baby's toes—if you happen to know a grey-green baby—have a transparent "window" at the top of each leaf to allow light to get into the heart of each toe.) We recommend only a very small meal (about one-half the strength recommended on the bottle) once a month for three months beginning in early March—and you know what happens then?

Blooms!

In fact, most Cacti and Succulents bloom.

To encourage growth of beautiful flowers on your Succulent, put it outdoors in a little early morning sun for a few hours a day until the first signs of color appear. The more common members of the family that produce showy blooms are Echeverias, Kalanchoe, and Crassula. One particularly fascinating group of Succulents is called Living Stones, the number one "Rock Group" of the plant world. They look just like what they're called, and in their usual state they sit in their pots and do nothing. But during the springtime, out of this ridiculous looking creature emerges an absolutely beautiful flower—practically certain outdoors, not so certain but definitely possible indoors with lots and lots of light.

There are at least fifty easily flowering kinds of Cacti and Succulents to choose from for indoor culture (easy for them, difficult for you!). But even if you were of a mind to read their names, there's no way we could possibly struggle through the job of spelling them. So because it's important you know the Cactus or Succulent you buy will indeed grow indoors, and because purchasing one is far safer than transplanting one found growing wild, a Cactus dealer is the best bet.

Well, that's about as far as we can honestly go. We know you'll come across many other books that will inform you that literally dozens (maybe hundreds) of other plants can be grown indoors—Geraniums, Dwarf Citrus Trees, Redwoods perhaps. We also know we've personally tried almost all of them, and with the exception of the plants we've talked about in this chapter, have had virtually no success. If you decide you want to gamble, just remember the immortal words of Julius Caesar—Caveat Emptor or something like that.

If you would like to know the names—and see pictures in both color and black and white—of virtually *every* plant in the world (Houseplants, Flowering Plants, Outdoor

The Original 15 Hassle-Free Plants

Plants, Cacti, Bromeliads—you name it, we mean virtually EVERY plant in the world), then we strongly suggest you start saving up for a very expensive, but almost totally complete Encyclopedia of Houseplants. It's called the *Exotica,* it's published by Roehrs, it costs somewhere between $70 and $80, and it weighs about 15 pounds.

Talk about heavy reading. . . . ❧

"I, Mr. Mother Earth, protest vigorously."

Originally, this chapter was to be called "Plants for Children."

But then we decided that a more appropriate title would be "Plants Are for Everybody" because we know from experience that plants can bring people together—adults and adults, men and women, men and men, adults and children, prison inmates . . . everybody!

What we are really trying to say is that the Plant Experience encourages growth in humans just as it encourages the growth in plants. Plants can give you a sense of inner peace as you marvel at their beauty and determination to please. They can also add to your sense of responsibility, and if worse comes to worse, they can give you something to talk about at parties.

Unfortunately, one of the last groups to accept the Plant Experience is MEN. Why?

Plants for Men

Well, over the years, a myth has been perpetuated that the care and feeding of houseplants is a hobby best suited for women or sissies.

I, Mr. Mother Earth, protest. Vigorously.

Feeling quite certain that I fall, at the very least, somewhere in between, and since it's no secret that I love houseplants, one of my main missions in life is to explode that myth. Hence, the battle cry of Mr. Mother Earth has evolved: MORE MEN IN THE MOVEMENT. (Actually, it's not exactly a battle cry, it's more of a plaintive wail.)

Everywhere Lynn and I go we find the houseplant experience is still mainly a woman's thing, although lots of men in the under-25 set are getting into the experience. But we're also finding that every day more and more men are admitting that they love houseplants and what-do-you-want-to-make-of-it, buddy?

Oh, we know it isn't easy to convert certain men over a certain age into plant people. The sissy myth is just too well ingrained. But how will you know if that plantless man in your life—be you male or female, and be he either a friend, a relative, a husband, a lover (or unless it's against the law, one of each)—until you at least *try* to get him involved in spite of his protests and seeming lack of interest? But how to get him involved?

Easy. Just follow this simple yet diabolical plan:

Buy him a plant for a gift!

*It's the only way a man
can have a baby, you know.*

Now before you say it would be a total waste, he's simply not interested in plants, "what he really wants is a new set of golf clubs—understandable since he just broke his last putter on the Fifteenth Anniversary of his inability to break 100"—meet us halfway and buy it as a non-occasion gift. You know, just a little remembrance because it's Wednesday, or whatever.

Make sure the plant you buy is one of the Hassle-Free ones in at least a 6-inch pot (6 inches in diameter across the top) so you know it's got a real good chance to live. (The larger the plant, the better its chances for survival, especially when it's under a pair of reluctant or inexperienced thumbs.)

Next, give the plant a name: Charlie, Susie, whatever you think might have some special meaning for him. Attach a card, "Hi. I'm Ming-Toy, your new Chinese Evergreen Plant. Please keep me in good, indirect light, water me only when my soil is dry, and most of all—LOVE ME."

Don't tell us it doesn't work. Oh, there may be a few half-hearted grouses at first, but you can bet those grice will turn to grins at the first sign of a new sprout from little Ming-Toy. (It's the only way a man can have a baby, you know, and with hardly any labor pains.)

There are a few other plants that for one reason or another are considered "masculine." Many Cacti and Succulents with their sculptured grace are appealing to men, as are Bromeliads, a fabulous species of plants that are as different from regular foliage plants as are Cacti and Succulents. These plants are particularly masculine in feeling and almost completely Hassle-Free. (If you want to learn the basics about Bromeliads, may we refer you to *Mother Earth's Hassle-Free Indoor Plant Book*? That particular section was written by the inimitable "Frenchy" DeLago, who encores with a chapter later in these pages.)

Another way to make a plant more appealing to a man is to plant it in an old tobacco tin, or an antique copper piece, or something else decidedly masculine in feeling.

By all means, stay away from ferny or flowery plants in trying to turn a man on. Not only are they difficult and therefore discouraging, but they'll arouse his memory of the sissy syndrome and you'll probably be finished before you begin.

We got a phone call once from a forty-year-old doctor, married, with three kids, who said he'd heard us talking about this Men in the Movement thing and thought he could help but he needed a private pep talk.

"Go ahead," said Lynn, flipping the little "The Doctor Is In" sign on her desk.

"Well," said Doctor X, "for about seven years now I've been growing African Violets. I've got over two hundred plants—most of which I've raised myself from leaf cuttings—and they're all blooming absolutely beautifully. . . ."

Lynn frowned. "So far it doesn't sound like you have much of a problem, doctor."

"That's what you think," he said. "You see, Lynn—all my Violets are in my basement, growing under lights. Nobody knows about them except my wife and kids, and they're sworn to secrecy because I've always been afraid if anyone found out. . . ." He was really choked up now. "Oh, how I'd love to find the courage to share them."

Lynn gave him the pep talk, crossed her fingers, and sure enough, about a week later, Doctor X called back.

He was ecstatic. He'd come out of the closet, so to speak, invited his friends over, confessed his secret, and was amazed to find that not one of them did anything but oooh and ahhh over the exquisiteness of the field of glorious color he had produced in his dingy basement.

All wound up taking home a plant, and the joyous doctor graciously offered to send us a very special thank-you gift—a Violet that had been thriving in his guest bedroom for almost seven years.

When we found out that this Violet was his mother-in-law, we respectfully declined.

Are you a bachelor who's down on your lady-luck? Or do you know a man whose "etchings" have simply stopped being a sufficient enticement?

Well—and we'll cite an example to prove it's true—plants can help your sex life! And you theirs (see Chapter 6).

Before you recoil at the prospect that we are about to get kinky, let us assure you that as fervently as we believe in having a relationship with your plants, we don't mean to imply you should . . . well, you know. What we mean is, a lonely bachelor will be delighted to find that once he loads his home with plants, he'll have little trouble finding

42

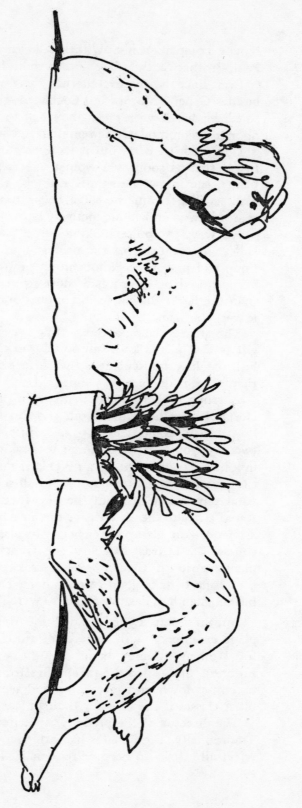

Plants can help your sex life.

female companionship. Witness the case of our brother Paul, Brother Earth as he's known to his intimates.

Ever since he discovered that there were other plants besides General Motors and Lockheed—the day he decided to fill his house with green—he's had to put in a revolving door to accommodate the feminine traffic.

Don't ask us why, but it works almost every time. We figure that as soon as a woman meets a man who loves plants, she knows he simply can't be all bad. (Naturally, plants will perform the same magic for women, too, but most hip women will instinctively know it.)

Anyway, if you're looking for a way to impress the ladies, hie yourself to the nearest nursery or plant boutique and pick up a Philodendron or Weeping Fig. You'll be surprised at how much more irresistible they can be than the latest shaving lotion or deodorant, and if the lady leaves, you won't be alone.

The greatest thing about getting—or giving—a plant as a gift is that plants know absolutely no class distinction. A lush, healthy houseplant is the perfect gift for anybody—rich, poor, male, female, young, old. . . . Example:

A group of geriatric patients from the California State Hospital were brought to our shop in the hope that the houseplants could turn on their interests again. About twenty people—most of them totally withdrawn—arrived in a bus accompanied by a psychiatrist and an orderly. All the patients were ambulatory and all seemed in relatively good physical health, but their eyes were glassy and they stared straight ahead. We gave them each a plant, and—like a miracle—the glassy stares began to disappear. Not all, of course. But at least fifteen of the twenty left holding their plants close to their bosoms, stroking the leaves, and promising to take good care of them. The psychiatrist was beaming, and, as best we recall, so were the plants.

Plants in the Pokey

Another time Lynn decided she wanted to share the plant experience with inmates of the California Institute for Women—a fancy name for the women's prison at Frontera. She called the prison director and said she'd like to come down and give interested women her series of plant classes if the director thought it would do any good.

The director of the prison was excited, but pessimistic. Traditionally, the inmates had a tendency to pair off and reject all efforts to become re-socialized; they didn't want

Clayton was potting plants
before he was potting himself.

to get involved in any project on a community basis. The director had tried several things, but nothing had worked.

Lynn, a female Don Quixote if ever there was one, decided this was a windmill she simply had to tilt.

So off she went about two weeks later to give her first plant class to a group of twenty-three women, most of whom probably just signed up as an excuse to escape a work detail.

The first session was the hardest. At the end of a rather nervous hour (after all, the girls were suspicious of Lynn's motives and Lynn was a bit ill-at-ease with them), Lynn asked them to write down the plant they would most like her to bring each of them on her next visit. When she got home and examined the cards she knew she'd been a hit.

Out of the twenty-three women, seventeen had written down Marijuana.

We're only kidding, of course, but the ultimate indication of her rousing success came not long ago in a letter from one of her original inmate students:

"You know, Lynn," Laura wrote, "when you first started coming here, I was skeptical of the results you'd get from the prison. But it was very beautiful to see each other turning on to plants. It brought a touch of feelings and warmth back to the women here. Most of us really miss our children—and our little plants are just like little children in a sense. We are really attached. Being here it's hard to show our emotions—but I've seen it all around me when we share our experiences with our plants. And that's something special."

Plants for Children

One of the most exciting things for anyone can be to turn a child on to the plant experience.

Perhaps you might feel that the instinct of a child would be to tear up or even eat the houseplants. But we can attest to the fact that by the time a child is four or five years old, he has only one objective when it comes to those pretty little green things in the house: to grow them.

It's a matter of exposure more than anything else. Children are born with an openness—a willingness—a desire, even, to love anything that's alive.

We have a nephew named Clayton who was making cuttings and potting them up before he was potting up what he really should have been. And Lynn has held her classes for dozens of schoolchildren who've come not knowing quite what to expect and then left as little plant freakettes. It's so gratifying when parents tell us that when they asked their child what he learned on that particular day, instead of the usual uninterested, "Nothing, really," they were treated to an almost word-for-word recital of the plant lesson.

There are, of course, certain plants which are better to start a child's plant experience with than others. Small children cannot and should not be expected to be as responsible or attentive to detail as an adult. Thus they really should get the hardy, easy-to-care-for little whipper-snappers at first, plants from the Hassle-Free list (see page 19). But since children have such fantastic imaginations, they're inevitably going to be attracted to the more unusual plants—plants that eat either flies or mini-hamburgers. Even though some of these plants will be difficult to maintain (like the Venus Flytrap or the Sensitive Plant), the children will be gaining some small scientific education so it doesn't hurt to let them add one or two to their collection.

A good way to start your child on the road to green-thumbdom is to substitute small plants for the ordinary party favors at his or her next birthday bash. It's amazing how much more excited a child will get over receiving a little 2-inch terra-cotta pot with a thriving plant in it rather than a plastic police whistle or a crummy glass-and-plastic ring. (This goes for children of all ages. Why not try the same thing at *your* next dinner party? Just be sure to tell your guests to transplant their new additions into 4-inch pots within a couple of weeks, since the plants can choke very quickly in these teeny pots for lack of root room.)

Another way to whet your child's appetite for growing plants is to demonstrate to him or her how easy it is to convert an ordinary coffee can into an absolutely beautiful planter to give as a gift. It costs almost nothing and will provide an added bonus of keeping the little tykes occupied for a few hours every now and then.

The operation is simple: Take a one-pound coffee can that comes with a plastic top (empty, of course) and with an ordinary "church-key" can-opener, punch four drainage holes in the bottom of the can. Next, spray the inside with

Use plants for party favors.

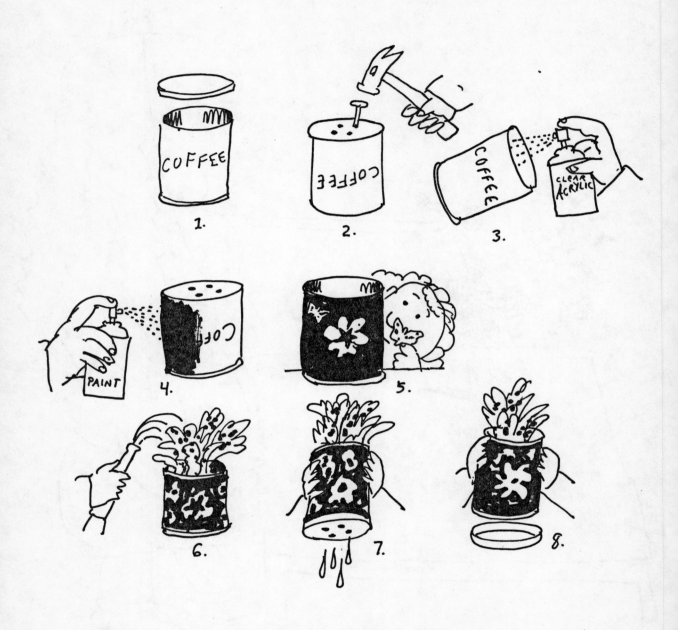

Coffee Can Planter

clear acrylic paint to prevent rusting, allow a few minutes to dry, then spray paint the outside any color you like, but preferably something bright and cheery. After this has dried, take a package of appropriate decals, available at drugstores or dime stores everywhere, and apply them to the painted can. Once planted, put the plastic top on the *bottom* of the can, and voila!—a stunning container that money cannot buy. For watering, remove the plastic bottom, allow the water to drain from the holes, then when it's drained completely, put the plastic back on again.

Oh, just one more instruction. Before you start, be sure to put lots and lots of paper down on the floor.

Specifically, what plants *are* best for children? Well, as we said, the hardies are best, but some of those unusuals that your child will inevitably want should be described.

Here are just a few:

Sensitive Plant (Mimosa pudica)—A plant with miniature locust-like leaflets that respond to the touch by folding up tightly and almost instantly. Needs good light, lots and lots of humidity, and the soil should be kept moist.

Venus Flytrap—A carnivorous plant which needs the high humidity found in a miniature plastic greenhouse or other terrariums. In its native habitat it feeds on flies, using its scent to attract them into its spiny jaws and then clamping the jaws shut and ingesting the fly. In captivity, the simplest and most sanitary way is to feed it teeny bits of hamburger about twice a week. (A friend of ours, a vegetarian, tried feeding his Venus Flytrap soyburger, an imitation meat dish. The plant rejected the soyburger summarily, but we weren't surprised. "What do you think that plant is," we asked, "a cannibal?")

Cobra Lily—Another carnivorous plant, which produces a flower in winter that looks like a cobra and smells like a pigsty, loves humidity so is best kept in terrarium-type conditions. Both for the sake of the plant and the sake of your nose.

Prayer Plant—The easy-to-grow Maranta is an ideal plant for children, not only because it requires only indirect light and a minimum of attention, but because of its lovely habit of closing up its leaves at night as if in prayer, a trick it originally learned in the jungles to catch the evening dew and absorb it. It should be misted daily to help avoid brown tips, and will grow for children of all denominations.

Morning Glories—Although not really a houseplant, it's fun for kids to plant Morning Glory seeds, put the pot in a sunny window, then watch for the inevitable sprouting and perhaps even a bloom in from two to three months. Morning Glories must be kept very moist and remember, they're strictly seasonal.

Other plants that are particularly fun for children are the smaller Cacti and Succulents, especially the Capped Cacti. These are little commercially-available Cacti that consist of rather ordinary green Cactus stems with colorful little "heads" that have been grafted on. (If you want to learn about grafting, you'll have to consult either a more scientific book on Cactus or your local plastic surgeon.)

Also fun are the do-it-yourself plants like avocados and sweet potatoes, which can be grown by simply inserting the bottom half in water, held up by toothpicks; or pineapples, which can be grown indoors by twisting (not cutting) the top off a store-bought pineapple, allowing it to sit out 24 hours to "heal," then placing it in water until little bitty roots appear. A container that keeps the light out is preferable while rooting. When roots are approximately 3 inches long, plant in potting mix and place in a bright sunny window.

Another idea that'll really turn on your kids—and you, too—is growing plants in water. Many tropical indoor plants will thrive in good old H_2O almost as long as they can in soil. Pothos, Nephthytis, Philodendron Cordatum, Chinese Evergreen and Wandering Jew are particularly good.

Next time you run across a particularly interesting bottle, instead of tossing it out or filling it with dried flowers, cut off a piece of one of the above-mentioned beauties with a razor blade, remove the lower leaves so you have a fairly long (4- to 5-inch) stem, place it in your container filled with warm water and a few pieces of activated charcoal and—that's it.

Have the child in your life feed the plant with a diluted plant food monthly—just a few drops, as you add new water only as the old water evaporates. Then both of you gaze in amazement as you see not only the leaves grow but the root system as well. (One of our neighbors, a 13-year-old girl, is growing a Philodendron in a huge Coca-Cola bottle. She calls her creation "pop" art!)

Actually, you'll find children getting into the plant experience even more quickly than your average adult—wanting to make cuttings, grow seeds—so just encourage them to try any plant they like, even ones that you feel certain will die. It certainly doesn't hurt for a child to learn a little more about life and death in this relatively harmless way, and as he gets older and more responsible he'll have greater and greater success.

We can see it now. A giant greenhouse someplace, bustling with activity inside, and outside, an equally giant sign:

"CHILDREN AT PLAY."

Even though we live in Hollywood and have a great many show-biz clients, we much prefer to stick to the greenhouse gossip and leave the movie star gossip to Joyce Haber or Ms. Rona, except for an occasional story like this one about Plants and Lucille Ball.

We have to tell you this story about Lucy for several reasons—not least among them that we hold her in complete and utter awe, not only for her immense and legendary talents as an actress, but for her incredible devotion to growing green things.

One summer not long ago, Lucy's son, Desi, Jr., had rented a house at the beach. In the middle of the summer, he was called out of town to work and was at a loss what to do with his plants while he was gone. He thought about giving them to his sister, Lucie—another confirmed plant addict—but he didn't want to shock them with a move, especially since he'd be gone less than a month . . . perhaps a professional plant service . . . ?

Oh, no, said Lucy. No stranger is going to take care of *my* grandplants!

So twice a week—despite the fact that she was working on a TV show, shooting a movie, and recuperating from a broken leg—she made that 30- or 40-mile round trip to Malibu to see that Desi's plants got misted and watered by someone they knew.

It is rumored that each time she left, the plants were heard to murmur:

"We love Lucy."

Well, doesn't everybody?

People who are successful with difficult plants
have either sophisticated gro-lighting, greenhouses,
or extraordinary luck.

As you know by now, we recommend you stay away from Glamour Plants (see Chapter 2) and virtually every blooming plant with the exception of African Violets or maybe (and it's a qualified "may-be") Geraniums. The people who have had success with these plants are definitely not the rule, although we have met them and they do exist.

Some people even manage to succeed with dwarf indoor Citrus Trees, but more typical is a call we got from a man who admitted his lime tree had been a lemon until he realized he had to put it on his patio so an insect could pollinate it . . . "My father never told me about the birds and the bees. He started right out with the men and the ladies. . . ."

The simple fact is that if you stay away from flowering plants for the indoors, you'll never have to sing the sad refrains of the famous old dirge, "My Fuschia Just Passed."

However, since it's almost certain that sometime in your life you'll either receive a flowering plant as a gift or be tempted to buy one for a friend, and because we know there's nothing that turns a person away from the plant experience quicker than two or three failures, it's vital you or your friend be aware that if something goes wrong it isn't your fault. The feeling you may have committed Plantacide is difficult to bear, so please—if nothing else—let these pages assure you that you bear no responsibility in the likely event your blooming plant doesn't make it.

Ah, you say, but how does one resist buying an Easter Lily or a Chrysanthemum or an Azelea or a Caladium, especially when they're so readily available and so frankly inexpensive in supermarkets and discount stores practically everywhere? Well the answer is one can't, we suppose.

So what snould you do with that Easter Lily or Chrysanthemum after the blossoms die? Or what about that magnificent Poinsettia you got for Christmas which has already begun to sag and wilt by New Year's? Or that gorgeous Mother's Day Gloxinia, or the scintillating Cyclamen you simply had to have?

Let's take these plants one at a time and investigate just what is the best procedure for keeping them happy and healthy after they seem to have "died."

Chapter 4.
Bulbs,
Holiday Plants,
and Some Blooming
Gift Problems

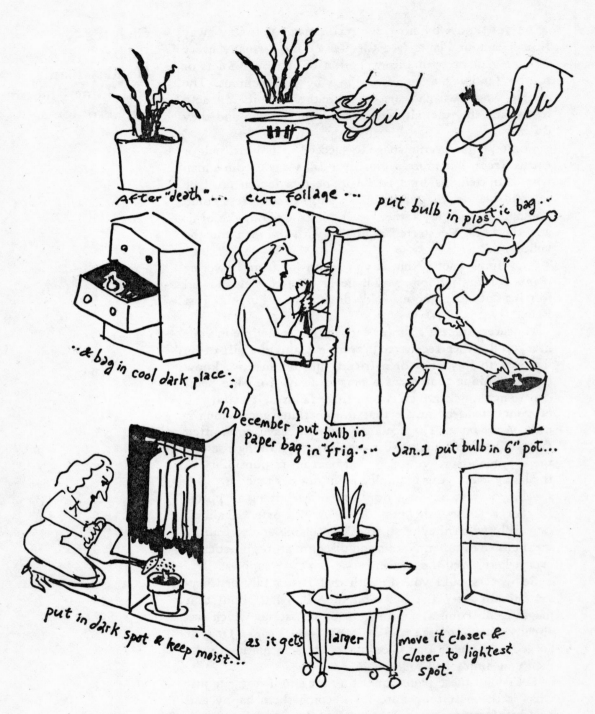

After "death"... cut foilage...

put bulb in plastic bag..

..& bag in cool dark place:

In December put bulb in paper bag in "frig.".

Jan.1 put bulb in 6" pot...

put in dark spot & keep moist...

as it gets larger

move it closer & closer to lightest spot.

Inside your home, bulbs need all the help they can get from Mother You.

(Incidentally, lots of people have asked us just exactly when a plant can be considered dead. The answer would be when its root system is no longer functioning, but since most of us can't be bothered with holding a mirror up to a plant's leaves or hooking an electrocardiogram to its roots, we suggest you can tell all hope is gone when there simply isn't a speck of green left and no amount of cutting back, watering and waiting can produce any.)

The first set of plants we'll deal with are bulb plants— the likes of Tulips or Easter Lilies, the two bulb plants you're most likely either to buy or receive as a gift, if for no other reason than they're the plants most commonly sold in supermarkets. (We're also talking about Gladiolas, Iris, Daffodils, Hyacinth, Caladiums, and Crocus, not quite as common but available in pots in most nurseries.) **Bulb Plants**

In their natural habitat outside, bulb plants bloom in the spring or early summer, "die" after a couple of months of growth, lie dormant for a year, then repeat the process with only the help of Mother Nature.

Inside your house or apartment, they need all the help they can get from Mother You.

Briefly, here's the best way to treat your bulb plant after the bloom has disappeared:

Wait for the plant to "die" (the foliage will wither and dry up). Then use scissors to cut the foliage off right down almost to the soil. It's okay to leave 2 inches. Remove the bulb from the pot, place it in a plastic bag, and store it in a cool, dry, dark place. A drawer will do fine.

Around the first part of December, put the bulb in the refrigerator in a paper bag. This way the bulb will know it's winter and therefore spring and it's re-blooming trip cannot be far behind. (Once we got a phone call on a radio show from a man who tried to put his Easter Lily bulb in the refrigerator in May, right after it had finished blooming. But alas, it didn't work. We suppose it was the bulb's way of telling him, "It isn't nice to fool Mother Nature.")

Around the first of January, remove the bulb from the refrigerator and plant it in a 6-inch pot, about one-third of the way down in the sterilized soil. (Our publisher, a true stickler for detail, would probably point out here that we forgot to tell you to take it out of the bag. So take it out of the bag first, okay?) Place the pot in a dark spot—in a closet, for instance—and water as frequently as necessary to keep the soil fairly moist to the touch. Keep a close watch on the plant until you see its first sprouts; then move it out of the closet to a place which is relatively dark, say the corner of a room which doesn't get a lot of light. Then as the sprouts begin to get larger, move it closer and closer to the lightest spot you've got, watering at least every other day. By the time it reaches Sun City, there's a fighting chance for some kind of bloom. Keep watering, keep waiting, and keep your fingers crossed. Maybe by Easter, you'll have a new Lily.

After all, Easter *is* a time for miracles, isn't it?

Blooming Gift Plants

Azaleas and Chrysanthemums are easily obtainable in supermarkets and do, in fact, make lovely gift plants, especially at the incredibly low prices for which they're sold. However, no matter how much light, luck, or desire you have, we just don't believe anybody can grow them inside. The next best thing is to keep your Mums and Azaleas bright and fresh for as long as possible. Keep them very moist. Water every day, spray with warm water, and rotate them as often as possible so that each plant gets a maximum of light. (We realize you might want to brighten up a rather dark corner with a blooming plant, so go ahead. Just make sure you've got a couple more so that you can rotate them and no plant has to spend more than a day or two in very dim light.)

Once the blooms fade away—and it's inevitable they will—the best thing you can do for both yourself and your plant is cut it all the way back to the soil and plant it outside in the ground. If you haven't got a yard and you haven't got a neighbor with a yard, cut it back and put it on a patio and water it a lot and maybe it'll grow back and bloom. If you haven't got a patio, either—no outside where you can put the plant to recoup or a friend with a suitable spot—then you've got to do something we know is very, very painful . . . plant it in the garbage can.

If you should happen to receive a Cyclamen or Gloxinia as a holiday gift plant, you have the famous two chances to keep it blooming: Slim and None.

But your chances will quickly leap to slim if (and this is especially true in the case of the Cyclamen) you live in a mild climate zone, for although both these plants need a

60

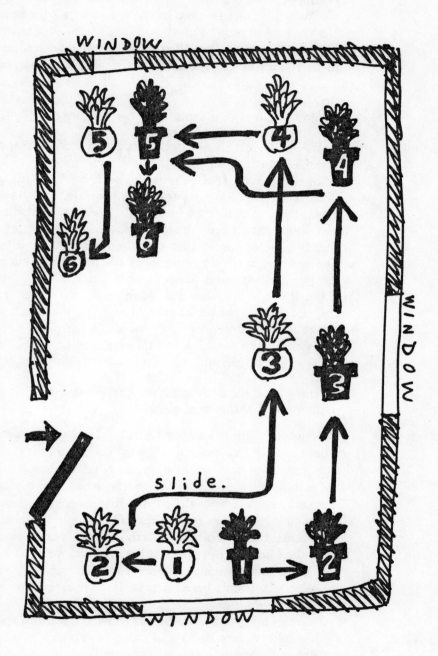

Rotate them as often as possible.

good deal of light and water to bloom, the basic single most important thing with the Cyclamen is to keep it *cool*.

Good luck. Blooms have happened in lots of cases. It could happen to you. But if it doesn't, and you have to send your Cyclamen or Gloxinia to Plant Heaven along with its Azalea or Chrysanthemum friends, be sure to save the pot, thoroughly sterilized with a hot soap-and-water bath.

Like the man said, it shouldn't be a total loss.

Cut Flowers

Speaking of total losses, let's take just a second to sneak in a word about cut flowers.

A question we often hear is "How can I keep my cut flowers fresh and blooming as long as possible?"

Well, there are lots of chemical products available at florist shops that'll keep those cut flowers fresh for quite a while, but we've found that just about the best and least expensive way is to add a couple of crushed-up aspirin and some purified charcoal to the *warm* water in which you put the flowers; keep the flowers in a light, cool spot; mist daily; and change the water every day.

What it boils down to is, if you call your plant doctor for advice on your wilting cut flowers, and he tells you to give 'em two aspirin and call him in the morning, don't get mad.

In this case it happens to be the best prescription.

Now back to things that grow.

Holiday Poinsettia

We suppose it just wouldn't be Christmas without Poinsettias. And let's face it, they're gorgeous with their flaming red or soft pink or creamy-white bracts. But they're not, in the true sense of the word, houseplants. (They are, in fact, Succulents, but that doesn't make any difference in how you should care for them in the house.)

The best thing about Poinsettias as gift plants is that unlike the Mums or bulb plants, for instance, you can keep your Poinsettia growing indoors for many, many years. And relatively Hassle-Free, at that. But remember, we said *growing*, not *blooming*.

After the original bloom begins to wilt, what you've got to do is take your scissors and cut your Poinsettia all the way down to about an inch from the soil, put it in the sunniest window you've got, start a watering procedure that ensures the plant won't dry out, then sit back and watch it grow.

Grampa Earth has transplanted his Poinsettia, which came to him in a 4-inch pot Heaven-only-knows-how-many Christmases ago, all the way up into an 8-inch pot where it's now a huge healthy foliage plant. But in all that time, it has never bloomed again.

And neither will yours, in all probability. Outside, in mild climates, in the ground in a spot where they get at least half a day of good sunlight, oh, my, is that a bract of a different color. Not only will your Poinsettias bloom in the spring, they'll bloom at Christmas, too, all the while growing into bushes of enormous proportions. But, we repeat, indoors, forget it. No bloom, no way. Not even the magic screams of Robert L. Green will make it happen.

One last tip about Poinsettias. That white sap you often see is very poisonous, so if you've got a child or animal who has a tendency to nibble on anything that looks like food, maybe you better try another kind of plant at holiday time.

We think Santa would understand.

Beware of poinsettia.

Mother Earth's Hassle-Free Hortoscope

We don't know how it is where you live, but in our neck of the woods the standard greeting to a stranger at most parties is:

"Hi. My name is Virginia. I'm a Sagittarius."

Since we don't know too much about astrology, we've discovered it's wiser merely to nod sagely when somebody launches into a discourse on why tomorrow is bound to be better than today because your moon is going to be in Leo, or your sun is in Pluto or your daughter is not in Venus or whatever. . . .

We don't mean to make light of astrology. It's probably just a natural defense mechanism to belittle something which has obvious significance but which one simply doesn't understand.

We *do* understand one thing quite clearly, however, and that is it simply isn't fair that signs of the zodiac all have symbols: Taurus the Bull, Virgo the Virgin, etc. They all have birthstones: Gemini, Emerald; Libra, Opal. But they don't have birth*plants*.

You guessed it. They do now!

But they probably wouldn't if we hadn't met Sabrina.

We were invited to meet some friends at a Halloween Party this past All Hallow's Eve. "It's going to be a great party. You'll love the hostess," they said. We arrived a little after 10—having stayed home long enough to hand out at least five dozen little plants in 2-inch pots to bunches of costumed and candy-stained trick-or-treaters—and were greeted at the door by a lovely, intense, dark-haired young woman wearing a long, black, flowing velvet caftan with a white satin astrological sign appliquéd to the front.

"Come in," she said, and we entered the dark, almost spooky-looking house, noticing at once the heavy smell of incense.

"My name is Sabrina," she said, stared at us for a moment, then: "You must be the plant people."

"Why, yes," we replied. "Have you seen us on TV?"

She shook her head. "I don't watch TV."

"Oh. Then you must be into ESP."

She shook her head again. "I'm into reading." She pointed toward our chests, and we smiled blushingly. We were wearing T-shirts that had *our* sign—MOTHER EARTH—appliquéd on the fronts.

"Actually," Sabrina went on, "I'm into astrology. Would you like me to make up your charts?"

"How nice of you. What will it cost?"

"One plant per chart," she said. "Preferably a Cordatum for the top of my bookshelf—doesn't get much light up there—and maybe a Spathiphyllum for a nice bright spot in my breakfast room."

"Hey," we said, somewhat surprised. "You're into plants, too!"

"I certainly am," Sabrina said. "Would you mind coming into my den for a couple of minutes? I'd like to talk to you about something you might find very interesting."

Sabrina's den was filled with lush healthy plants, and we nodded admiringly.

"Your plants look sensational," we said. "Have you any special secrets you may have plucked from the planets?"

"As a matter of fact, I have. I give all my plants a birthday—the day I bring them into my house—and then I treat them according to the needs of their particular astrological signs."

We looked at each other. We had heard of a parapsychologist who kept his plants alive at a distance of 3,000 miles by meditating on them for half an hour every day, but this was about as far-out a method of plant care as we'd ever come across.

"Amazing," we said. "That's all you do?"

"Oh no," replied Sabrina. "I also follow all the advice you give in your book." She moved across the room and began to stroke the fronds of a billowing Boston Fern. "I've been thinking," she said. "Why shouldn't there be birthplants of the zodiac?"

Once again we looked at each other. "Sounds interesting," we said. "How would it work?"

"Quite simply," she replied, taking down three or four rolled-up, yellowing parchment scrolls from a bookshelf crammed with tomes on astrology.

"What I thought I could do," she said, unrolling the scrolls, "would be to describe the major qualities of each sign, and then let you decide which plants fit best in which sign."

And so it came to pass.

Remember, we've tried to be faithful to the yellow parchment scrolls, thus some of the birthplants are Hassle-Free, some are Almost Hassle-Free, and a couple . . . well, for them, longevity in the house was just not written in the stars.

So here it is, on regular paper since parchment is *really* in short supply—The Mother Earth Hassle-Free Hortoscope!

Aries, the Ram (March 21 to April 20)—You're a Ram, (unless by the time you read this you've been traded to Green Bay or jumped to the other league). Mars is your ruling planet (and frequently your favorite candy bar), Tuesday's your lucky day, and your birthplant is the ever-popular Cleopatra Begonia.

Why? Because Sabrina's parchment scrolls indicate that Ariens are fiery, energetic, impulsive, excitable and exciting. And the entire Begonia family fills that bill. (We picked the Cleopatra because it's our particular favorite, but actually, when buying a Birthday Plant for an Arien friend, you may select any Begonia you wish.)

The Begonia family can be divided into three parts: Wax, Rex, and Tuber. (Sounds like a great vaudeville act, doesn't it?) All are considered to be blooming plants, especially outdoors in temperate climes, but of the three,

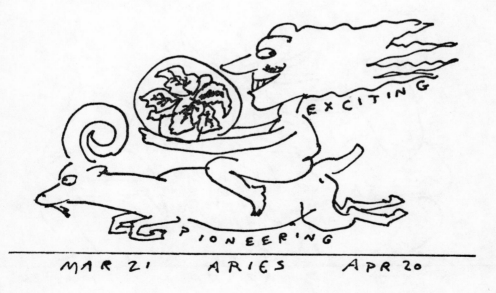

MAR 21   ARIES   APR 20

67

Rex and Tuberous are really much more valued for the fiery, energetic, and exciting foliage that as Ariens they impulsively produce. And we mean impulsively, for growing these beautiful creatures indoors without the incessant worry of their leaves' drying and curling up can be a very tricky business.

Ariens are truly the Pioneers of the Zodiac, and Begonia people are probably the foremost Plant Pioneers, forever striving for new and more brilliant hybrids. It has been our observation—not to mention the advice from a high-ranking member of the American Begonia Society—that the most beautiful Begonias (outside of greenhouses) are cultured in terrarium-type surroundings: large glass bowls or aquariums, covered either by plastic-wrap or (in homes with careful children) by a snug-fitting plate of glass.

When grown indoors they prefer a cool bright room, their soil damp and good humidity (provided by other plants surrounding them, a dry well under the plant filled with water each day, or if you are really serious about growing Begonias indoors, you really should have a humidifier. We found ours at the local drugstore for around $12. Yes, it's small but it does work nicely if you are looking for just a bit more humidity in a small area.) Remember the green golden rule: Don't mist plants with hairy or fuzzy leaves, and this certainly applies to the beautiful Begonias.

APR 21   TAURUS   MAY 20

Taurus, the Bull (April 21 to May 20)—Your ruler is Venus, your birthstone is diamond, your color is blue, and your birthplant is the Staghorn Fern.

A pretty obvious choice. In the first place, the Staghorn looks exactly like its name: A spate of olive green, slightly fuzzy leaves grow out and up in the shape of horns, much more majestic that any bull's horns, but horns nonetheless.

But it is more than just the obvious that prompts us to designate this magnificent creature as your birthplant. According to Sabrina, Taurians have a strong sense of preservation. And according to us, so does the Staghorn. It is an epiphytic plant, one that affixes itself to a "host" (a tree or a rock in its natural habitat—usually chicken-wired onto a redwood board in captivity). Unlike a parasite, however, it does not live off the host, but takes its moisture and nutrition from the air. Stubborn, dogmatic, slow—all these traits are prominent in Taurians, and in Staghorns, too.

They are slow growers hung outdoors in the shade or indoors in a cool light spot. For best results indoors or out, spray every day or two, and see to it that the root system and host are given a thorough watering or dunking at least once a week. Your Staghorn Fern should hang in there until it reaches a hornspread of as much as 6 or 7 feet across.

Staghorns reproduce themselves by sending out small plantlets, or "pups," at their bases. These puppies are great gifts for adults and children and are very easy to wean from their mother. When the pup plant is 4 to 5 inches high, clip off at the base where it's attached to the mother plant, using a very sharp knife. It's just as painless as cutting the umbilical cord, but not as necessary because the pup can remain with the mother endlessly. Fetch a piece of redwood bark (the pup is too small to play fetch), cover the root system with sphagnum moss, wire the pup and moss firmly to the board, and water thoroughly.

How many pups might you expect during the lifetime of your Staghorn Fern? Well, because Venus has given you Taurians a sex drive even those daily showers and weekly dunkings can't suppress, we can only say that properly cared for, your birthplant will give birth many times during its long and fruitful lifetime.

Gemini, the Twins (May 21 to June 20)—Your ruler is Mercury, your baseball team is Minnesota, your birthstone is Emerald, and your birthplant is Piggyback.

Before we proceed, let us add that among your signmates are Mr. and Ms. Mother Earth.

Yep. We're both Geminis, and to tell the truth, we're very chauvinistic about it. Not that we don't think the other signs are good, mind you. It's just that ... well, when you've got it, flaunt it!

And *that* the Piggyback does. Kept in a good, light spot and watered frequently (a small amount every day won't hurt), the Piggyback plant produces miniature leaflets on the back of every leaf—thus its name and incredible popularity with plant lovers all over the country.

This double personality, so to speak, is typical of all Geminis and also indicative of their absolutely unsurpassable ability to create. (Remember, we *said* we were Gemini-chauvinist Piggybacks!)

Like all Geminis, your Piggyback will be quick to criticize but quick to forgive. For instance, if you don't water him enough, you'll walk into his room one day and find him hanging there totally limp and apparently dead. However, if you take him outside to a nice shady place and water him thoroughly, he'll pop back up as beautiful as before within a couple of hours.

Frankly, Sabrina assured us that Geminis will have better luck with Piggybacks than people of other signs. You see, she said, since the Gemini person (and Piggyback) is Versatile, Clever, Witty, Exhilarating, Entertaining, ad infinitum, he obviously needs the company of someone or something equally perfect lest he die out of sheer boredom.

Alas (and we hated to hear this, even though we suspected it), Geminis are not known for their ability to sustain any relationship or interest on a permanent basis.

There are just too many things to do. Thus, although we've talked to people who've been able to keep their Piggyback thriving for years, we've also found that a year or two is the most you can really expect out of your relationship.

The tendency in most Geminis (and Piggybacks) is to try to run off in all directions, to grow long and leggy, as it were. The Gemini will unleash his truly brilliant creative powers only if forced to slow down, so pinch back the plant frequently. That'll help keep him full and bushy and around for a much longer time.

We know first-hand. All Geminis like a little pinch now and then.

Cancer, the Crab (June 21 to July 20)—Ruled by the Moon, your color is maroon, Moonbeams will simply leap

JUNE 21   CANCER   JULY 20

off your Moonstone and you'll go Moony over your birthplant—Moodenhair—that is, Maidenhair Fern.

Because you're sensitive, sympathetic, motherly, easily influenced, crave sympathy, expect a great deal of love and attention, and changeable, it simply couldn't be anything else. But alas, don't Moon around too much if your birthplant doesn't make it in the house because, although there are exceptions, Maidenhair Ferns are just too delicate. They need a greenhouse or ideal outside setting to do their glorious, breathtaking best.

We must confess that a gorgeous Maidenhair might just be the most beautiful of all plants—but one that isn't making it inside . . . that's another story. What usually happens, even when you find a nice, light, cool place, water frequently, and provide the plant with the maximum humidity possible (most people try their Maidenhairs in their bathrooms where humidity from showers is generally fairly good), it will soon start turning brown, then dry up and wither away and you'll think the plant is "dead."

Stop! Notice the quotes around "dead"?

Here's where you have to treat it like the Cancer that it is. Smother it with attention, give it all the sympathy it craves, cut off those "dead" fronds all the way down to the top of the soil, take the pot outside, put it in a shady area, water it frequently, and if you've done your job with the right amount of sensitivity, your Maidenhair Fern might just be around for your next birthday! If *you* live!

Leo, the Lion (July 21 to August 22)—This is another fiery sign, as well it should be, being ruled by the Sun. If you're a Leo, your color is purple, your birthstone is ruby, your mane is probably too long, and your birthplant is the Croton.

Your plant is just like you and Sabrina—proud, energetic, outgoing—and the use of subtlety is the only way to best this beast.

Crotons are temperamental, and although in tropical places such as Florida or Hawaii they grow wild and flamingly brilliant, colors of pink, red, yellow and green emblazoned in absolutely surrealistic patterns on their flat, sometimes broad, sometimes thin leaves, they are really very difficult to maintain indoors. The sun lends to the Leo a happy vibrant disposition, just as the sun helps keep

ENERGETIC

PROUD

ARROGANT

JULY 21   LEO   AUG 22

the Croton's colors brilliant and alive. If you're to have any chance of keeping your Croton from dropping its lower leaves indoors, however, you're going to have to create a tremendous humidity while at the same time make sure your Croton/Leo is getting plenty of light and a shot of food every two weeks. Plant food, that is, not raw meat.

If you can manage to create enough humidity by constant spraying and keeping your Croton on a saucer filled with pebbles and water, you might be rewarded, as Lion/ Croton is noble and proud, and will, if properly motivated, absolutely be King of your indoor jungle simply because he's got a built-in arrogant love of display.

Incidentally—and it makes one wonder where astrology ends and witchcraft begins—Sabrina the Leo has eight Crotons—every one of them in the pink . . . and green, and yellow, and red. . . .

Virgo, the Virgin (August 23 to September 22)—You're ruled by Mercury, you're definitely the Earthy type (although how an Earthy type stays a virgin is a little hard to understand), your birthstone is sapphire, your color is gray, and your birthplant is Sansevieria.

When Sabrina described the essential qualities of the Virgo native, we knew at once that nothing but Sansevieria could possibly fit the birthplant bill. Exact, meticulous,

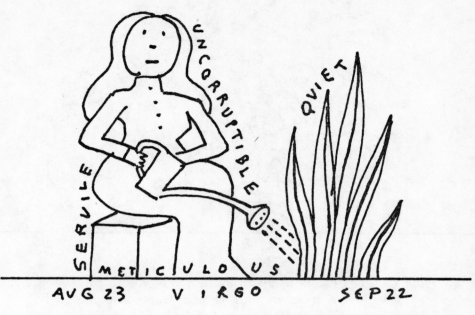

SERVILE UNCORRUPTIBLE QUIET METICULOUS

AUG 23 VIRGO SEP 22

painstaking, intelligent, a compulsion to serve, quiet, unsentimental and virtually incorruptible.

Given the botanical knowledge that virtually every form of Sansevieria will thrive indoors or out, in the dark or in strong light, needs water only when the soil feels dry, grows slowly but steadily virtually forever, and is a stark, unadorned, straight-ahead plant—don't the characteristics seem inexorably intertwined?

We don't know how you feel, but when we told Irving, our Sansevieria, he was a Virgo, the old pragmatist didn't visibly turn a leaf. But inside we knew he was most satisfied.

Libra, the Scales (September 23 to October 22)—You're ruled by Venus, your color is blue, your birthstone is opal and yours is the very Sign of Marriage. (The Sign of Divorce, incidentally, is $$$$.) Your birthplant: any member of the stately Dracaena family.

Venus, your sign ruler, endows you with a huge variety of attractions, as it does your birthplant. (There are dozens of varieties of Dracaenas, each one more striking than the next.) Libra is also the sign of supreme cooperation, and providing you keep your Dracaena in fairly good, indirect

74

light, water only when dry, manicure the tips from time to time and be aware that all Dracaenas are stalk plants (that is, their lower leaves eventually fall off, leaving long, tall, terribly interesting looking trunks with a tuft at the top), you'll find your Dracaena will cooperate completely.

(Sabrina laughed when we told her we'd picked the Dracaena as the Libra birthplant. Pointing to a beautiful Dracaena Marginata in a corner of her living room—a lovely, curving, airy-looking plant—she told us, "That plant's name is Harvey, after my first husband. He was tall and skinny without much upstairs, and—you guessed it—he was a Libra.")

Harvey notwithstanding, Librans are considered intelligent and artistic, and the Dracaena family certainly meets these requirements. Artistic, anyway, since their ever-growing, twisting stalks usually manage to wind up looking like brilliant modern sculptures. And come to think of it, the only Dracaena we ever knew that could be classed as unintelligent was a certain Massangeana who simply couldn't understand it was supposed to have a bright chartreuse stripe down the middle of each broad green leaf and kept growing pale-green stripes instead. ("Still sounds like Harvey," said Sabrina.)

Finally, Sabrina told us most Librans are careless about money matters, so we advise you never to give your Dracaenas a penny more than they absolutely need.

SEP 23   LIBRA   OCT 22

MYSTICAL ENERGETIC PASSIONATE

OCT 23 SCORPIO NOV 21

Scorpio, the Scorpion (October 23 to November 21)—
Born under a water sign, your color is brown (appropriately becoming our planet's new water color), your birthstone is tourmaline, and there seems to be some confusion as to whether your ruling planet is Mars, Pluto, or Goofy. There is no confusion, however, about your birthplant—the Spider Plant.

Lest you feel we took the easy way out and picked a Spider Plant because a spider would seem an appropriate match-up for a Scorpion, that's not absolutely true.

We picked Spider for Scorpio after realizing that one of our best friends is a Scorpio, and he has a bushy, green and white striped crown with long, cream-colored runners dangling down, at the end of which are little miniature green-and-white plantlets. Seriously—

The traits of a Scorpio/Spider: Energetic (look at all those babies it tosses out), Passionate (has to get all those babies somehow, right?), and Mystical (how does it get all those babies?).

Scorpions are in a constant state of evolution and regeneration, just like the Spider Plant, and, too, Scorpio's feelings are generally directed toward people, rather than things.

You'll simply have to believe that every Spider Plant we've ever known is deeply interested in people and simply couldn't care less about things.

76

SAGE IMPULSIVE INDEPENDENT FIERY

NOV 21 SAGITTARIUS DEC 21

Sagittarius, the Archer (November 22 to December 21)—Let's try a little change of pace on this one. We'll give you the astrological highlights and then see if you can guess the birthplant, okay? As soon as you think you know the answer, push that little button-mushroom and shout out your birthplant loud and clear.

Sagittarius is ruled by Jupiter by Jupiter! and is an extremely fiery sign. Yes, Contestant #3. What? No, it's not a Chili Pepper, but better luck next time. To continue:

Sagittarius is considered the sign of the counselor, or sage, and his independence, his love to be free, is vital to his happiness. Anybody? It shouldn't be hard, contestants. You've already read about this plant in an earlier chapter. . . .

Sagittarians are mostly impulsive and impatient, have a love of traveling. . . . Yes, #1? Creeping Charlie? Oh, such a good try . . . but that's not it.

Maybe if we tell you how to take care of the plant, it might make it easier. The Sagittarius birthplant needs to be in very good filtered light, pinched back frequently to maintain fullness, and watered when dryish.

Yes, sir? Coleus. Now, sir. If you'd been paying attention you'd have remembered that Coleus likes to be kept *moist*.

This plant does very well on its own. It can—listen closely now—carve a home out of virtual wilderness . . . to repeat an earlier clue, it loves to TRAVEL.

Did we hear somebody say that the Sagittarius birthplant is a Wandering Jew?

Give that person a map to his nearest nursery, and we'll see you next time on "You Bet Your Aspidistra!"

Capricorn, the Goat (December 22 to January 20)—Ruled by Saturn, your color is black, your sign is an Earth sign, and your birthstone—oh, this is rude—is zircon. Well, perhaps because Capricorn's a goat, the birthstone people were afraid it might eat its birthstone, and heaven forbid it was anything valuable. . . .

But as for us, the birthplant people, we recognize, thanks to Sabrina, that Capricorn is a very prestigious sign. To be specific, it occupies the Tenth House of honor, prestige and career, and as far as we're concerned that entitles it to have a Most Honorable Birthplant: the Inscrutable Chinese Evergreen.

As Capricorns, Chinese Evergreens are persevering and tenacious. Their actions are well ordered, and through hard work they are generally able to move slowly but inexorably upward. As goats, they also need frequent baths.

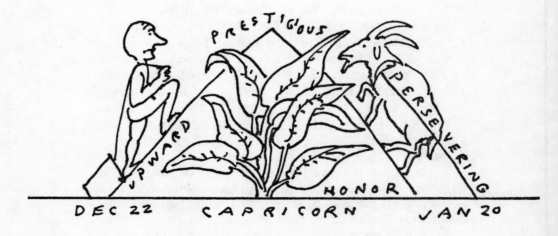

DEC 22   CAPRICORN   JAN 20

78

Really. It's a good idea to wipe down your Chinese Evergreen—in fact, practically all your plants but Ferns—with a mild, hot, soapy solution (a biodegradable dishwashing liquid) at least once a month.

The infinite variety of Chinese Evergreens available (Treubii, Pseudo-Bracteatum, Schismatoglottis, etc.) makes it possible to have an entire houseful of nothing but this one species and yet seem to have a collection of fifty or sixty different kinds of plants.

As for care, just indirect light and water when dry.

However, Sabrina tells us, since they're Capricorns, your Chinese Evergreens probably won't be very good lovers.

Oh, well. No plant is perfect.

Aquarius, the Water-Bearer (January 21 to February 19)—Ruled by Uranus, Aquarius (which sounds to us like a water sign) is actually an air sign. Oh, well, we're not here to bicker with the house astrologer. Your color is electric blue, your birthstone is amethyst, and your birthplant:

Ivy!

How we arrived at this one we really can't say. It just came to us, sort of like a vision from the stars, and we decided not to take issue with whatever greater force sent it to us.

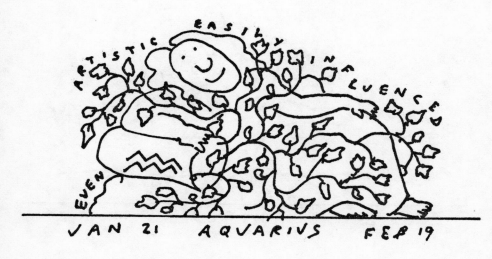

JAN 21   AQUARIUS   FEB 19

Maybe you'll get the same vision if we tell you that the Aquarian is artistic, easily influenced, popular yet solitary, and has a wonderful even disposition.

Baby Snooks, our favorite Grape Ivy, who sits in her antique barber chair near a window in our living room, has every one of those qualities. Maybe that's why we flashed "Ivy" when Sabrina gave us the astrological side.

So if you're an Aquarian, consider yourself an Ivy.

Try to consider yourself a Grape Ivy, because no matter what anybody says you'll be happier indoors in pretty good indirect light than will your brethren—English Ivy, Glacier Ivy, Needlepoint Ivy—all beautiful but just a wee bit happier outdoors.

Just one last piece of advice. Even though you're the Water Bearer, don't drink too much. You prefer to be kept on the dryish side.

Which is maybe why you're an air sign after all.

Pisces, the Fish (February 20 to March 20)—Well, astrologically speaking, this one really comes together. It's a water sign, ruled by Neptune, and its color is sea-green. So right away we suggested to Sabrina that we make its birthplant the Sea Onion, or the Shrimp Plant, or even Charlie the Tuna, the World's only Suicidal Fish.

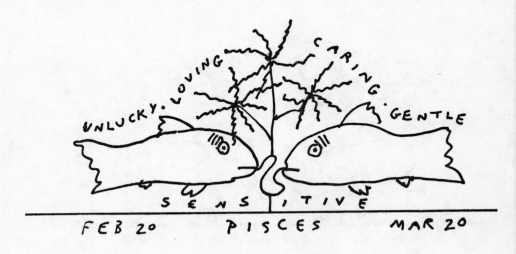

Wait, she cautioned, until I tell you what kind of plant you have to seek: It must be gentle, sensitive, unlucky and, most especially, need someone to love and care for it.

Wow, we realized. The Pisces plant would have to be something special. And then we knew. Aralia Elegantissima, a graceful dark green plant that looks—well, frankly—like Marijuana, but if it were only as easy to grow. . . .

It's another one of those Glamour Plants that's probably going to lose most of its lower leaves no matter how much good light and humidity you can supply indoors. (Outside, of course, it'll grow just as easily as that weed we mentioned earlier.)

The Elegantissima is hard to resist because of its tall, feathery, graceful look, but unless you're an exceptionally strong companion—a typical Pisces trait—you might not have the greatest luck in the world with your birthplant.

We understand that in certain Pisces there's a strong tendency to turn toward drugs or alcohol for escape when things go bad, so if you're a Compleat Pisces, better just admire your birthplant from afar.

So there they are.
The Twelve Stars of Mother Earth's Hortoscope.
Sabrina asked us to mention just one more thing.
In the event you don't like the particular plant we've picked for your birth sign, go ahead and change it to any other you like.
Good Karma, she said. Or something like that.

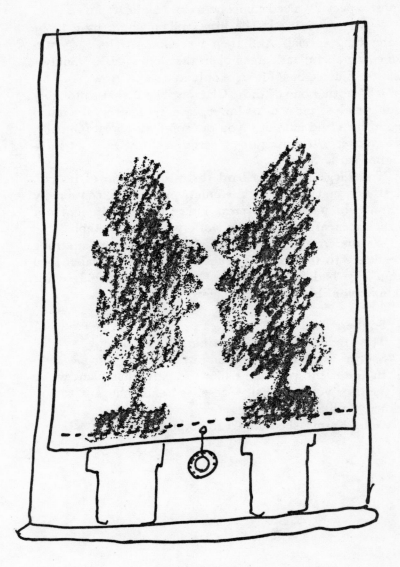

Propagation

For quite a while, we were hesitant to include a chapter on Propagation.

For one thing, we felt it might be too scientific for a Hassle-Free book. Also, because propagation obviously has to do with reproduction (i.e., S—E—X), we were afraid a chapter of that sort might change the rating of the book from G to X.

But since most of you are no longer total amateurs, and since everybody seems to be much more broad-minded about subjects of this sort these days, we're going to risk it.

Besides, one of the greatest joys of the plant experience is to Grow Your Own, whether it be plants you can eat, plants for your home decor, plants to turn on a friend (and we mean by giving them cuttings, not by making funny little cigarettes), or whatever.

Watch what happens when you really get into propagation. You'll find yourself trading cuttings with friends and discussing, etc. Eventually you will *ask* a friend for a cutting of a particularly nice plant that can spare it, because plant people get as much pleasure from giving cuttings as getting them. In fact, you might even find yourself trading cuttings through the mail with out-of-state plantoholics. (We once snapped a twig from our neighbor's jade tree, but it was a huge plant and right next to the sidewalk and needed pruning anyway and we gave it a good home, and yes, Your Honor, we know it's called stealing but since it's our first offense . . . What's that, Your Honor? If we send you a cutting you'll drop the case. . . ?)

One of the most exciting success stories of "amateur" propagation came to our attention a few weeks ago.

We got a call from a friend of ours named Barbara who had bought a very beautiful Pothos plant from us about four years ago. It was a rare, large-leafed variety which was growing on a pole and was about 3 feet tall. We reminisced about how Barbara had agonized over spending $12.50 for a plant—admittedly rather expensive in those days for a Pothos, but this *was* a championship specimen, so she finally took the plunge. Now she wanted us to come over and see how her investment had grown.

Chapter 6.
Propagation,
or Plant Parenthood

It needed pruning anyway.

When we walked into her living room, our jaws dropped. There, in a nice, light, airy spot, was a Pothos plant, growing up a stick, at least 8 feet tall and fully 5 feet in diameter. The Pothos to end all Pothoses. A plant from a horror movie entitled *The Pothos That Ate Pittsburgh!* We were aghast . . . dumfounded. . . . Was that . . . ?

Barbara nodded. One and the same. By regular feedings, pinching back, and a lucky combination of plant-and-spot, she had created this exquisite monster. And that wasn't all.

She led us to another room. So help us, lined up on shelves and sitting on saucers all over the floor were at least thirty more of this rare, huge-leafed Pothos variety, each at least 2 feet in height and each full, lush, and gorgeous.

"Each of these is from a cutting off King Kong out there," she said. "And you know what? I've been selling them for $10 apiece!"

Knowing a bargain when we see one, we immediately produced a tattered sawbuck and offered it to Barbara for one of the plants.

"Don't be silly," she said. "Be my guest. Take one."

We were hesitant, but Barbara quickly put us at ease.

"Please help yourself," she said. "Since you once owned the father, under all rules of plantdom you're entitled to pick of the litter!"

So let's take a leaf from Barbara's book—or better yet, her Pothos—and start talking about the specifics of this rewarding and fascinating indoor sport—Propagation.

Everything You Ever Wanted to Know about Cuttings but Were Afraid to Ask

There are two different types of propagation by cuttings: Leaf and Stem.

Stem cuttings are the ideal way to propagate such plants as Philodendron, Pothos, Ivy, or Wandering Jew. Merely cut off a piece of the parent plant with a single-edged razor blade about one-quarter inch below a leaf node, or joint, and dip it in a good commercial rooting hormone. Although many people recommend plopping the cutting into a glass of water laced with a bit of purified charcoal, then waiting for roots to form before planting it in potting mix, we prefer to root cuttings in vermiculite, a nonorganic rooting medium. We have found that roots grown in water are thicker and more succulent than those produced in a denser mixture, and when planted in soil, may fail altogether.

Leaf cuttings can be taken from African Violets, Succulents, Begonias, Geraniums, Piggybacks, and the Peperomia family. The process is virtually the same as in stem-cutting culture. Cut the leaf off with a sharp knife, retaining as much of the stem as possible. Dip the leaf into a rooting hormone to prevent rot. Then plant the leaf about a quarter of the way down in vermiculite. That's right. Just stick it in the pot. For quicker results, cover your rooting container with glass or a plastic bag to help create a miniature greenhouse and higher humidity, which will actually be visible as waterdrops inside the baggie. Once roots have formed (you'll know because you can take out the cuttings once a week to check on their progress), transplant cuttings into individual pots of potting soil. Have patience. Sometimes it takes weeks.

The Air-Layering Report

Air-layering is a more complicated operation than rooting cuttings and is used most successfully with such plants as Dracaenas, Rubber Plants, and Dieffenbachias. If these plants—all of which have a tendency to lose their lower leaves and grow into tall, rather bare stalk plants—become unsightly to you, the next step is not weeping, wailing and gnashing of teeth. No, it's air-layering. *Then* you have an opportunity for weeping, wailing and gnashing of teeth.

Actually, the operation is really no more complicated than a tonsillectomy. Begin by removing a strip of bark directly below a *node* (the "pimple" where a leaf grows out of the stem), and then cut a notch, preferably with a single-edged razor blade, about one-third of the way through the stem. Check the patient's sap-pressure and root-beat, rub the wound with rooting hormone, then insert a matchstick or toothpick into the notch to keep it open, wrap the entire cut and stick with damp sphagnum moss, tie with string or "plant ties," and wrap with a plastic bag. You'll have to check the plant to make sure the moss remains damp and to see when new roots show through the moss. Then sever the plant just below the root formation and pot it. "Blade! Nurse!" You can then cut the stem into smaller pieces, dip them in rooting hormone, lay them on their sides in vermiculite, and when plantlets

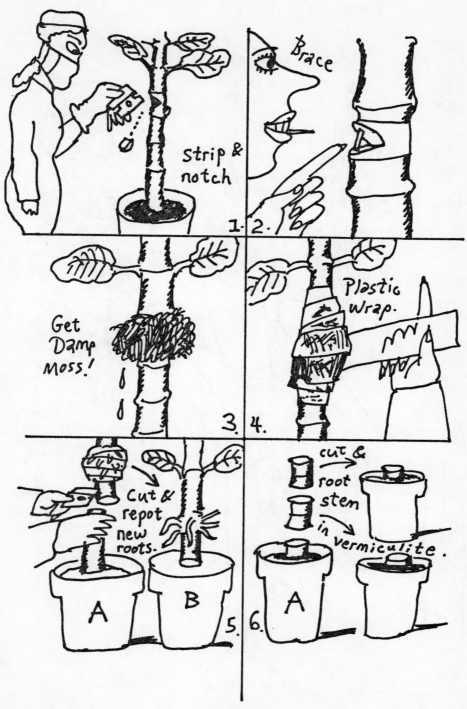

Air-Layering

"Deep Division"

form on the ends of stems, plant them. Come to think of it, not such a complicated operation after all. What's more, you don't need an anesthetist.

Small plants that appear at the base of an old stem are called suckers, or offsets. (P. T. Barnum said, "There's a sucker born every minute." But try and tell it to Gertrude, our favorite Bromeliad. Since the day we brought her home over two years ago, she's failed to produce even one baby. Oh, well. Gertrude only cost $3. Think how bad the people who bought Secretariat feel!) Anyway, suckers or offsets also appear on other members of the Gesneriad family, such as the Trichosporum, or Gloxinia, and fibrous-rooted Begonias, as well as Bromeliads. To plant an offset, simply cut it off the mother plant with a very sharp knife or single-edged razor blade, dip in rooting hormone, and pot it in potting mix. If it cries for the first few nights away from its Mama, just put a clock in its pot.

The Happy Sucker

Stolons, or runners, are small plants that dangle free from the mother plant. Most commonly seen on the Spider Plant, the Strawberry Begonia, and the Piggyback, these little plant-tots can be removed by using scissors to cut them off just above the top of the plantlet, and then planting them in potting mix if they already have roots, or rooting them as stem cuttings if they don't. Within a month the latter should be ready to be planted in potting soil.

Any Stolon Can

African Violets, cane-stemmed Begonias, Succulents, Ferns, Sansevierias and Bromeliads—any plant with more than one stem emerging from the soil—can be propagated by division.
First remove plant from pot. (If this seems difficult, break the pot first by laying it on its side and tapping gently with a hammer.) The next step is cutting directly through the roots and soil with a very sharp knife or gardening tool, removing the separate divisions, and then planting them in potting mix. Give them a thorough watering with a vitamin/hormone mixture, but don't fertilize for one month.

Deep Division

Now we all know that plants can "feel" pain, so if you're worried about performing this surgery, we hasten to assure you that if you work quickly and confidently and speak soothingly to the plant as you go, it'll hardly feel a thing. Like parents removing a splinter from their child's finger are apt to say, division will hurt you worse than it'll hurt your Fern. Remember that all plants suffer a bit from transplant and change—as do people—so don't expect too much for about a month while they come around.

The Sensuous Seedlings

Although any plant that flowers can be started from seed—and that includes practically every plant in the kingdom—it's really not very practical to think in terms of growing indoor plants from seed. However, because there are lots of Herbs you might want to try in your kitchen window, or perhaps a Citrus or Papaya, we'll outline some basic principles of how you can discover that as you sow, so shall you reap!

Seeds should be sown sparingly (three to four per 6-inch pot) and evenly in the top one inch of a starting mixture of equal parts sand and peat moss, then covered by just a wee bit more soil than the depth of their own size. The soil must never be allowed to dry out, and if possible, be kept at around 72 degrees. When the seedlings first begin to show above the soil, move the pot to a brighter light, making sure they get no direct, hot sunshine. Once active growth begins, feed every two weeks with diluted liquid plant food (about half the ordinary feeding strength found on the bottle), and then transplant the seedlings before crowding begins.

The Joy of Sporing

Spores are found on the back of Fern fronds in masses of small, round, light circlets in precise design. As soon as the spores have matured—you'll be able to tell because they'll turn a deeper brown color and can be removed easily—clip an entire frond and place it in a closed paper bag to ripen. Once the frond is ripe (begins to dry and turn brown), remove the spores by shaking them off, and sow them in a mixture of equal parts garden loam, sand, peat moss, and leaf mold, or packaged indoor potting mix or sphagnum moss, covering the entire pot with a pane of glass or a tightly pulled piece of plastic wrap. It is vital that spore plantings be kept moist, so set the pot in a saucer of water until the plantlets have grown to a height of 2 to 3 inches. Then transplant them into 2-inch (in diameter) pots.

CLIP A FROND WHEN SPORES MATURE · RIPEN IT IN A CLOSED PAPER BAG.

SOW SPORES IN POTTING MIX · KEEP MOIST UNTIL READY FOR TRANSPLANT.

The Joy of Sporing

Have you noticed an upsurge recently in the number of packaged sprouts available in your supermarket? Besides being a tasty vegetable eaten raw, sprouts can be enjoyed in salads, sandwiches, vegetable dishes, and omelettes, imparting a delicious flavor and an interesting crunchiness. They are so rich in vitamins and minerals that a person could live on sprouts alone for several months, and they're super for all of us dieters. Best of all, you can eliminate the middle-man by purchasing the beans (or seeds) and sprouting them yourself.

**The Games
Bean Sprouts Play**

91

Hybridizing

The best place to hatch a sprout is in the kitchen, away from bright light (although sprouting can be enjoyed on camping trips as well). The most common beans for sprouting—mung, soy, garbanzo, lima, kidney, navy and pinto—are available at health food stores. You can also sprout the seeds of alfalfa, mustard, sesame, barley, oats and garden peas. Finally, you can even sprout pumpkin seeds, squash seeds and a couple of nuts—almond and pea.

Cover several dozen beans (or a handful of seeds) with water, making sure they are not too crowded in the container, which should have a cover of either plastic, china or glass to keep the air out. Change the water in the container every day for four days, and if you have ordinary luck, a majority of the beans will have sprouted to a harvestable length, which varies with every bean or seed and can best be determined by your taste buds. Harvest by cutting off the sprouts with scissors.

Sprouts are fun for the whole family, and since children can grow them by themselves, you're liable to see your children not only eating but loving a food that is "good for them."

For a comprehensive guide to sprouting, we suggest you pick up a copy of *The Bean Sprout Book* by Gay Courter. Meantime, if you'll excuse us, we have to go check on our bean bag chairs. One of these days they're just bound to sprout!

Hybridizing —or Open Marriage

Only God can make a tree. But a Plant Freak, with lots of patience and proper greenhouse conditions, can create new forms. The science of hybridizing is too special to try to relate here, but once you reach the state in your plant experience where you want to start inventing plants of your own—be they a new form of Bromeliad or a new colored Violet—you'll surely find plenty of literature to guide you down this glorious path.

And besides, we're beginning to get a little uncomfortable about this discussion of the Sex Life of your houseplants.

After all, what two adult Dieffenbachias do in the privacy of their own pots is really none of our business, is it? 🐛

When our publisher suggested we include a chapter on Bonsai in this book, we were hesitant.

In the first place, Bonsai is very much a Japanese Art (although there are thousands of non-Japanese Bonsai hobbyists), and our knowledge of things Japanese was pretty much confined to those ridiculous clichés of old World War II movies—or modern TV auto commercials.

And more importantly, we didn't know the second thing about Bonsai!

We did know the *first* thing: Bonsai is the art of stunting and shaping trees and plants in small, shallow pots. And an "art" it is, if you've ever seen one of these incredible living sculptures.

Would it be fair for us to dispense advice on such a difficult and specialized affair?

"No," agreed our publisher, "but since Bonsai is an Ancient Japanese Art, why not find an Ancient Japanese Bonsai Artist and let him dispense it?"

And so find him we did.

His name is Mr. Yamamoto (his wife calls him George-san), he owns a small Bonsai nursery, and he's been creating prize-winning Bonsai trees for years.

Our first encounter with Mr. Yamamoto was a bit embarrassing.

Mrs. Yamamoto had a great deal of difficulty understanding our mission, but finally she nodded smilingly and indicated that George-san was working in the back of the second lath-house.

Lynn was marveling at some of the incredible specimens spread on tables all around us as I took off toward the back, hoping that the three years I spent writing "McHale's Navy" would help me with my pidgin-Japanese.

Mr. Yamamoto was bent over a potting table, trimming the roots of a small Juniper Tree, preparing it for Bonsai. I spoke with some trepidation.

"Mr. Yamamoto. . . ?"

He turned—a handsome man in his early sixties, his piercing dark eyes staring at me, waiting.

I bowed slightly. A good touch, I thought. "Sayonara," I began, then quickly: "I mean, Ohio." (Those words I had picked up during an exotic visit to a neighborhood Japanese restaurant.)

Chapter 7.
Mr. Yamamoto
Talks about
Bonsai

All Bonsai must be kept outside.

"Ohio," he replied, returning my bow.

"Us"—I pointed to myself and Lynn, still browsing through the Bonsai wonderland in the background—"wife-san, Lynn, and me—write book." I held up a copy of our first book, then raised two fingers and went through a series of gyrations meant to illustrate what I was trying to say.

Nothing.

As I stood there trying to figure out how to break this communication barrier, Lynn walked up, beaming with joy, just having wandered through a virtual Bonsai forest... miniature trees, gnarled and twisted plants, mostly all irregularly branched with low, horizontal growths and thick trunks.

"Mr. Yamamoto," she gushed, "I simply can't tell you how absolutely beautiful your plants are!"

He bowed, and smiled for the first time. "Madame," he said, speaking the most perfect English I'd heard since my last Ronald Colman movie, "a compliment from one such as you is doubly meaningful and I am deeply appreciative."

I stared, open-mouthed. "You... you speak English...." I stammered.

"Quite proficiently, Rapp-san."

"Well, I'll be..." I laughed uneasily. "I suppose you attended one of our major universities...?"

Mr. Yamamoto smiled patronizingly and shook his head. "I took my higher education at Oxford." He turned to Lynn. "I understand you're interested in gaining some information on Bonsai?"

"We'd certainly appreciate any help you could give us." Lynn prodded me out of my state of shock.

"Huh? Oh, absolutely. Like I said, we're writing another book, and—"

"As I said," Mr. Yamamoto interrupted. "Like I said is incorrect. But forgive me. It's nit-picking, an unfortunate habit we English majors find difficult to break. Please continue."

We decided the best way to find out what we wanted to know was simply to start our tape recorder, ask Mr. Yamamoto all the questions we had ever been asked about Bonsai, and then, when the taping was through, edit out what wasn't necessary.

So here is the transcript of that tape, but for reasons students of history will understand, we didn't edit out anything.

US: Mr. Yamamoto, what exactly is Bonsai?

MR. Y: Bonsai, or "tray trees," have been used by the Japanese for about ten centuries. Basically, most Bonsai are from 12 to 26 inches in height, although some specimens can grow to almost 4 feet. Since most are easily carried in one hand and one might be tempted to keep his Bonsai indoors, it must be remembered that a Bonsai's home is outdoors.

US: Got it. Now, in regard to what plants make the best Bonsai—

MR. Y: *With* regard. A common error.

US: *(Sheepishly)* Of course. Anyway, what plants do make the best Bonsai?

MR. Y: The coniferous evergreens are probably the most popular of all trees for Bonsai. Junipers in particular are recommended to the beginner as they are very easy to train.

US: That's odd. We had a Juniper once that was still wetting the carpet at the age of six!

MR. Y: Nice try, Rapp-san, but let me continue. Spruce are also easy to grow, but you must keep in mind that *any* plant can be Bonsai—trees, flowers, fruits and grasses—as long as it can be kept in scale with its container.

US: Really?

MR. Y: Most assuredly. It has been said: "The materials for Bonsai are all around us, even in our own gardens. But we won't see them unless we are under the spell of the tiny trees."

US: How poetic! Written by a Bonsai expert from Tokyo?

MR. Y: No, a Mrs. Schwartz from Burbank, one of my best customers. Come. Let me show you some of my most prized specimens. Here for instance is a prime example of Kabumono style Bonsai—a pot containing a single plant from which may spring any number of trunks but four.

US: Why's that? Three's company but four's a crowd?

MR. Y: Because the Japanese word for four—*shi*—sounds like another word which means death.

US: Ahhh, very wise. Helps keep the plant from passing on to that Great Geisha-House in the Sky.

MR. Y: Western humor continues to fascinate me. Much in the manner of a train wreck. Ah, here is a magnificent specimen. A prime example of Chokkan.

US: Chokkan? Is that the name of the plant?

MR. Y: No, of the classification. Chokkan means "upright trunk"—a single tall tree standing proudly in level country.

US: That sure is a beauty. Can we call it "Chokkan Delight"?

MR. Y: You *may*—not can—call it anything you wish. Ahhh—here is one of my favorite plants—a maple growing in the Shakan form—that is, a slanting trunk imitating a tree growing at right angles to a mountain slope. This plant is nearly twenty years old.

US: Amazing. It doesn't look a day over sixteen. Mr. Yamamoto—forgive us for asking—but your prices are . . . well, a little high, aren't they?

MR. Y: Not at all. Bonsai trees can range all the way from as low as $5 or $10 for newly begun plants to as much as $3,000 for a plant such as this maple—and even many thousands more, depending on the age and shape of the specimen.

US: Wow! We should have listened when mother told us to become Bonsai experts! But what if a person can't afford to purchase a Bonsai tree but does have a yen (forgive us) to make one himself? Do you think you could give us a brief explanation that might help a beginner to understand?

MR. Y: No.

US: Beg your pardon?

MR. Y: A brief explanation of the art of Bonsai would be impossible.

US: Well, wouldn't you please try? You know what they say: The difficult takes a while, so the impossible takes a little longer.

We should have listened
when mother told us
to become Bonsai experts.

MR. Y: Very well. One must begin by digging up or purchasing the plant of his choice—be it a coniferous tree, a deciduous tree such as a maple—a species, incidentally, which is considered the most poetic and elegant because of the way it captures the essence of each passing season; or, perhaps, a flowering plant such as an Azalea or Chrysanthemum—although flowering plants are usually selected from the wild species. To be honest, however, I would recommend that the neophyte purchase his plants in the beginning.

US: At these prices, we don't blame you!

MR. Y: The prices to which you refer are for specimens which have already been stunted and shaped. The price of a small plant for do-it-yourself purposes is quite nominal.

US: Of course. Once our budding Bonsai buff has bought his baby, what then?

MR. Y: He must then cut off the roots to the barest minimum so that the plant can be placed in a very small pot and its growth stunted.

US: He couldn't just puff a little cigarette smoke onto its twigs, huh?

MR. Y: It is fortunate my Bonsai work has given me infinite patience and an indefatigable calm. Once the roots have been cut and treated with a commercial root conditioner to prevent the plant from suffering shock, the plant must then be put into a bed of sandy loam in an unglazed training pot.

US: Training pot? Wouldn't it be simpler just to wrap its roots in rubber panties? A small joke. . . .

MR. Y: Virtually infinitessimal. Once planted, it must be sprayed frequently, kept in partial shade, and in two or three years it will be ready to be transplanted into an appropriate Bonsai pot where it must be tended and established for another year before the tedious process of shaping begins.

US: Good heavens! It takes longer to become a Bonsai than a Doctor!

MR. Y: Which explains why the cost is so dear. Once the

shaping process is complete—and because to verbalize this process would be a painful task and would make, frankly, dull reading, your readers will have to seek out any of the multitude of excellent photographic books on the subject if they are interested in further pursuit—the plant can be put outside almost anywhere. Only in the intense heat of summer or in the very coldest weather should a Bonsai be moved indoors for longer than a day or two.

US: We know lots of people get Bonsais as gifts or would like to buy them for themselves but are afraid to try. Could you give them a little basic information on watering and feeding quickly?

MR. Y: Of course, but first I must chide you on your use of a misplaced modifier. The schedule of watering depends entirely on the nature of the plant's root system, its age, location, and the season. Some may be watered a few times a day, others once a week. A general rule is to wait until the soil is half-dry before watering. With regard to feeding, a Bonsai should be fed every three or four weeks during the spring and summer with a low-nitrogen houseplant food.

US: Anything else we should know?

MR. Y: We have barely scratched the surface. If you would really like to learn much from a book, may I recommend one which rather thoroughly covers the subject of Bonsai, and includes some excellent photographs?

US: By all means. Then we could recommend it to our readers.

We followed Mr. Yamamoto back to the main section of the nursery, where he took a book from his private shelf.

"I consider this an excellent text on the subject. Please take it as my gift."

He handed us a copy of *Bonsai: Miniature Trees,* by Claude Chidamian.

"Mr. Yamamoto," we said, "we are eternally grateful." We gave him a copy of our book in return, and although he bowed respectfully, we thought we saw him wince. "Is there any last piece of advice you'd like to leave our readers with?"

"Yes," he said. "Never end a sentence with a preposition." He grinned sheepishly. "I fear I have caught your rather odd sense of humor. Seriously, if one is interested in learning the art of Bonsai, it is best, if at all possible, to locate a genuine Japanese Bonsai Nursery and then pay a visit for a person-to-person talk, or even better, a demonstration of how Bonsai is done."

"An excellent idea," we said, "but where would one look for the name of a Japanese Bonsai Nursery?"

"In the Yellow Pages, of course," he said, and then turned and walked back toward his potting bench. ❧

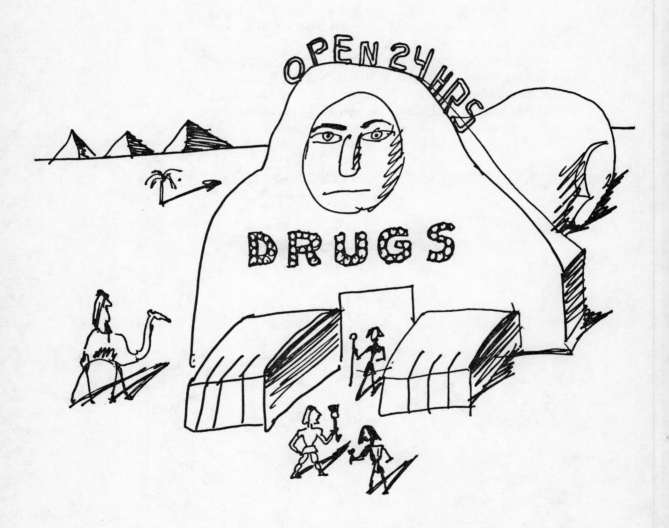

*Early mankind discovered
that certain plants contained
medicinal properties.*

The scholarly looking diploma over Lynn's desk reads "MS. MOTHER EARTH, P.D."

Plant Doctor, that is.

We do our best to minister to our ailing houseplants. We even try hard to diagnose over the phone, but we don't for a minute want to pretend that we're qualified to diagnose or cure diseases of Homo sapiens.

There are, however, some pretty well-established rules with regard to the treatment of both external and internal problems with plants and Herbs, so we'd like to pass some of them along.

Herbal medicine is quite logical. After all, how many doctors do you think they had back in prehistoric times? Do you suppose there was a Mayo Brothers' Clinic in 1572 that consisted of twelve tepees and an X-ray machine?

Early mankind, by means of trial and error, accidents, etc., discovered—often the hard way—that certain roots, plants, barks and seeds possessed medicinal properties.

The world's oldest medical literature dates from the 2nd Century B.C. in Egypt and is called the Papyrus Ebers. Among those Herbs employed as remedial agents were myrrh, cumin, peppermint, caraway, fennel, olive oil and licorice. Licorice, among thousands of other Herbs, was also mentioned in a book on medicinal Herbs written by a Chinese emperor about 3000 B.C. (Licorice is also mentioned by our daughters about four times a day.)

The Romans, Persians, Babylonians, Greeks, Arabs, Hebrews, our own American Indians, and early colonists were also well acquainted with the use and practice of herbal medicine.

Most recently, large drug firms in the United States and Europe are re-reading old books on herbal medicine, and financing costly expeditions in search of roots, leaves, barks, and seeds. For instance: The Indian plant Snakeroot (Rauwolfia) has been used for thirty centuries by the natives to alleviate nervous depression. Not long ago, Western researchers uncovered its potent source, reserpine, and began to market it. A drug company executive commented:

"We finally figured that ten million Indians couldn't be wrong."

Chapter 8.
℞: Plants
(Plants for
Medicinal and
Cosmetic Usage)

Remember earlier we mentioned that some of the information in this book—especially in this chapter—wouldn't be of the same practical nature as, say, how often to water a Philodendron or when to transplant a Tradescantia? We also, if you remember, said we were going to pass it along anyway, because we felt it was entertaining and informative, and "fun" can be every bit as important a medicine as "ginseng." Besides, almost all of the plants discussed below can be bought, processed, at any good health food store. So don't expect to learn how to grow these medicinal Herbs and roots; just expect to get acquainted with their names, what they can do, and if you do pick up something along the way you can put to practical use, then, by all means, run, do not walk, to your nearest caldron and brew up the plant panacea of your choice!

Alfalfa—used as a treatment for arthritis when the powdered Herb is taken with cider, vinegar and honey: One teaspoonful of each in a glass of water. (Come to think of it, there are very few cases of arthritis recorded in the horse world, so it probably is a pretty practical remedy at that!)

Aloe Vera—the sap of this common succulent is excellent as a remedy for blemishes and burns. We have quite a few—Aloes, that is, not blemishes.

Asparagus—yep, the juice of the root of the common asparagus has been long used as a sedative. Try it sometime—have asparagus for dinner and see if you don't fall asleep that night!

Basil—may be used for brewing tea as a treatment for nervous disorders. Also can be used as a first name for someone wishing to portray Sherlock Holmes.

Catnip—relieves pain when infused one ounce to one pint boiling water. Also, for the many of you who have called or written to complain you can't keep your cat away from your houseplants, Catnip is your best hope. A potful near his litter box will keep him occupied and as far as relieving pain is concerned, it'll certainly help relieve the pain of your gnawed-on Palm Tree!

Cayenne—considered the purest and most positive stimulant in the herbal materia medica. Also useful as the base for sneezing powder.

ALFALFA · ARTHRITIS

ALOE · BURNS

ASPARAGUS · SEDATIVE

BASIL · NERVES

CATNIP · PAIN

GINSENG · EXHAUSTION

MOTHERWORT · VAPOURS

OATS · INSOMNIA

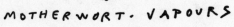

Dandelion—the common, pesty weed, dandelion, is actually quite useful in the treatment of liver and kidney disorders. The roasted roots may be ground and substituted for coffee if yellow coffee is your bag.

English Walnut—infusion of one ounce bark to one pint boiling water remedies both fever and skin diseases. (At least that's what it said on the tag under our coffee table.)

Ginseng—15 grains immediately after meals aids in relieving mental exhaustion. "The Chinese Panacea," Ginseng is currently the hottest selling herbal remedy in America.

Kelp—excellent source of iodine for imbalanced diet. Sold already processed in most health food stores. Also a major troublemaker for fishermen trying to reel in their lines.

Motherwort—according to one old English researcher, one-half to one dram of this powdered Herb "takes melancholy vapours from the heart and leads to a Merry, Cheerful and Blithe Soul." (Mother-love will also accomplish the same thing, wethinks.)

Oats—believe it or not, the liquid extract of common oats can be used to treat insomnia. (Some of the sleepy horses we've bet on obviously haven't had their oats before the race.)

Hold everything! Stop the presses! Sometimes very amazing things happen—like, just now, while we were working on this chapter, we heard the plop of our morning paper on the front porch. We stopped to peruse it quickly, and would you believe—on the front page of the *Los Angeles Times,* the biggest story of all was headlined: "FOLK MEDICINE—MAGIC ASIDE, MEXICO HERBS OFTEN WORK."

Fantastico! It related the wonders of a typical morning at the herbal and magical stalls of the Sonora Market in Mexico City—fifty stalls dispensing curative wares, the literal center of Mexico's enormous trade in "traditional" medicine. Founded in the 16th Century, this "street of herbal stalls" dispenses the same medicines dispensed by the ancient Aztec Indians.

We learned that the shell of an armadillo costs $3.20, and boiled, it produces a brew to fight whooping cough.

Mother-of-pearl shells are used as receptacles for lemon juice, the juice absorbing special properties from the shell, then the resultant liquid is used to clear up the complexion. The biggest seller is ruda, an Herb that clears up indigestion; another popular Herb is enojo, which fights colic.

The "magic" part? Well, according to the *Times* report, the old Aztec doctors always accompanied the administration of the Herb with "a good deal of incantation, ritual, and exorcism that, in the long run received more credit for the cure than the Herb. The same is true of Sonora Market. The merchants sell amulets with as much fervor as they sell Herbs. It is hard to separate the medicine from the magic."

Far out.

Okay, herbal-tea break over. Back to the drawing board.

Pine Oil—used as inhalations for bronchitis and laryngitis, or as an ointment for eczema.

Primrose—infusion of the leaves and root into a salve heals wounds and aids in the treatment of muscular rheumatism.

Rosemary—this easily obtained Herb, combined with borax will (and remember, we're only quoting from our research) prevent premature baldness and make an excellent hairwash. Culpepper, the universally known Olde English Herbalist, said: "If a maid is curious as to her future she may obtain information by dipping a spray of Rosemary into a mixture of wine, rum, gin, vinegar and water in a vessel of ground glass. She is to observe this rite on the Eve of St. Magdelene in an upper room in company with two other maids, and each must be less than 21 years old. Having fastened the sprigs to their bosoms and taken sips of the tonic—sips are quite enough—all three go to rest in the same bed without speaking. The dreams that follow will be prophetic." Good Lord, Master Culpepper, don't you know we only deal in Hassle-Free things?

Silverweed—steep weed in white wine or vinegar and then apply to skin for treatment of pimples. (Notice unnecessary instruction to use *white* wine? Any connoisseur knows you never drink red wine with Silverweed.)

Sunflower Seeds—used in bronchial, laryngeal and pulmonary infections, coughs and colds. The recipe we found:

ARMADILLO - WHOOPING COUGH

PINE OIL - ECZEMA

ROSEMARY - BALDNESS

SILVERWEED - PIMPLES

SUNFLOWER · COLDS

WITCH·HAZEL · STY

WORMWOOD — MOTHS

W A H O O · CONSTIPATION

"Two ounces Sunflower seeds and one quart water boiled down and strained; add 6 ounces sugar and 6 ounces Holland's gin." Huh? Six ounces gin? With that kind of recipe, you don't need the Sunflower seeds!

Wahoo—eliminates constipation due to inactivity of the liver. (You must admit, it's aptly named!)

Witch Hazel—ointment made by adding one part fluid extract bark to 9 parts simple ointment used as local application for treatment of sty in the eye. Pie in the sky? You be the judge.

Wormwood—essentially used as a moth repellent for clothes. Also an ingredient of vermouth. (Maybe what happens is the moth gets drunk, passes out, and thus leaves your woolens alone.)

Literally hundreds more Herbs are considered to have medicinal or cosmetic values. If you're interested in knowing the names of them all, there are many excellent books on the subject, one of which is *Proven Herbal Remedies* by John H. Trobe.

To reiterate, we can't guarantee any of the medicines we've listed will actually work. We're almost 100 percent positive, however, that none of them will hurt you. So if you feel like becoming the Euell Gibbons of the Medical Set, why not give it a try?

In the meantime, we're going to eat some asparagus and take a little nap.

Born to be eaten.

It was about 1 o'clock in the morning when the phone rang, its shrill clanging practically jarring us out of bed. Since Lynn prefers the side of the bed away from the phone (in the event of just such happenings as this, I suspect), I was forced to pick it up.

"Hullo . . ." I mumbled sleepily, praying it wasn't one of our plantochondriacs calling up with a story of a sick Philodendron.

"Dolling, congratulations!" It was Frenchy, our 75-year-old mechanic friend and well-known Bromeliad freak.

"For what?" I mumbled, trying to think what Lynn and I could possibly have won, especially at this hour.

"Godzilla just had six catlets. Four boys and two girls!"

"That's great," I said, coming a bit more awake now. "But how come congratulations for me? I never laid a finger on that cat and you know it!"

Lynn, who was now up and leaning across to listen in, poked me in the ribs. "We gave Frenchy Godzilla and her husband Chitty, don't you remember?"

"Oh, of course! I guess that makes us the kittens' godparents, huh?"

"That's right, dolling," Frenchy said. "Loretta says you should come over for dinner tonight and see them and I'll cook up some onion soup, okay?"

"Okay," I mumbled, hung up, and went back to sleep, not exactly sure I was happy to have been partially responsible for adding six more cats to the burgeoning world feline population, even though they were pure-bred Russian Blues.

We got to Frenchy's about 6 o'clock that night, and he greeted us at the door in his familiar jumpsuit and beret, absolutely beaming with excitement. Somehow not exactly the picture of a genuine gourmet cook—but in Frenchy's case, one smell is worth a thousand words.

"Wait till you see them," he crowed, and led us to the bathroom where his wife Loretta was gazing down into a cardboard box. There, each busily slurping away at one of Godzilla's drinking fountains, were six teeny little grayish things—distinguishable from rats only because Frenchy and Loretta assured us they were kittens.

"Aren't they beautiful?" Loretta asked.

Chapter 9.
Born to
Be Eaten

117

Lynn leaned down and looked at them adoringly. "They're the cutest things I ever saw."

"What do you think?" Frenchy asked me.

"They're nice," I said. "But I'm allergic to cats."

"Come on, then," Frenchy said. "You can help me pick the Herbs for dinner tonight."

As we walked through his Bromeliad forest toward the back of his yard, I frowned.

"I didn't know you were interested in Herbs," I said, pronouncing the "H" in Frenchy's—and the European—manner.

"Are you kidding, dolling? I've always liked Herbs. Except Herb Hoover. A chicken in every pot! There were days I would have settled for the feathers!"

By now we'd reached an area in the back of the yard where pots and pots of Herbs were set out on a table. As Frenchy started clipping bits and pieces of this and that to use in seasoning the meal, I noted that each individual pot was labeled as to its contents, and in addition, the table was divided into three groups of pots—one group labeled "Condiments," another "Spices," and the third, "Herbs."

"What's the difference?" I asked.

"Between feathers and chickens?"

"No, between Herbs, Condiments and Spices."

"What's the matter with you," he frowned. "Didn't you ever read the dictionary?"

"Oh, I started it once, and I admit there were some pretty terrific words, but the story was boring, and—"

"Okay, Mr. Mother-Smarty-Pants, I'll tell you the difference. According to D. Webster, a Condiment is a pungent substance such as salt or pepper; seasonings. A Spice is any of various aromatic vegetable products such as nutmeg, cloves, curry, etc., used in cookery to season foods. A Herb is a seed plant which does not develop woody persistent tissue, but is more or less soft and succulent, used for medicinal purposes or for its sweet scent and flavor. Anything else you'd like to know?"

As I watched Frenchy clipping shoots off a Rosemary plant, then harvesting a small pot of Chives, moving down the table to snip off a handful of fresh Tarragon, all the while sniffing his fingers and ecstatically savoring the fresh pungent aromas and obviously bursting with joy at the prospect of seasoning his dinner with Herbs and Spices he had grown himself, I realized I had found an important answer to what had been a nagging question:

What should we do about the chapter we had planned—but not yet written—on Herbs?

At first glance, this would seem like a simple question with a simple answer:

Write it!

But, alas, nothing is ever quite so simple as it seems.

You see, in spite of the fact we're well aware that whole books have been written on the subject of Herbs, Lynn and I have always felt everything that really needed to be said could be said in a few concise paragraphs, such as:

"Many Herbs grow wild in the United States. All grow wild someplace. If you're lucky enough to live in an area where Herbs grow wild (and you're educated enough to know one from the other), then by all means, whenever you get the chance, harvest them by cutting off as much as you can carry home, use what you can that night or the next day for maximum freshness, and then chop up the rest, dry it, grind it and put it in tightly capped jars for future use.

"If you don't live where Herbs grow wild, but you have a backyard, plant Herb seeds (available at all nurseries), following the directions on the packet as to what kind of soil is best, how often to water, how often to feed, when to plant, when to harvest, etc. Then harvest and do the same thing with regard to using and drying as you would with Herbs you capture in the wildwoods.

"If you don't have a backyard, but you do have a patio with some good sunlight a few hours a day, almost any Herb, planted either from seed or cutting, will grow in containers outdoors, either in pots or planter boxes. All you'll need to know is when to plant the seeds, how to plant them (see Chapter 6 on Propagation), how much sunlight, if any, they need, how often to water, and when to harvest. All of this information will be available on the packet of seeds that you buy.

"Finally, if you want to grow Herbs inside, probably in your kitchen window, you'll have two choices: You can go to your nursery and buy Herb seeds, sow them, take care

"Won't eating plants hurt your image?"

of them according to the packet, and so on. Your other choice: You can buy Herb plants already pretty well established in 3- or 4-inch pots, and if you put these in the kitchen window, keep them relatively moist and harvest frequently, you ought to do pretty well."

And that's it, or so we thought. Any more information would be superfluous, especially in a book like this. Except of course to steer you toward the five or six or seven Herbs that are the easiest to grow indoors and steer you away from a few that are extremely difficult.

But as I watched Frenchy clipping and snipping and sniffing and loving, I realized that in a book like this the main thing was to try to impart to you the feeling of joy that using Herbs you've grown yourself can give you. That feeling of accomplishment we talked about before. And even more, in a book like this we could give you the opportunity of hearing of this joy from someone unique and entertaining and knowledgeable and interesting. We could make—with Frenchy's help—the chapter on Herbs and cooking with Herbs a genuine entertainment.

"Frenchy," I said, in awe of having discovered yet another of his seemingly endless talents, "would you please write the chapter on Growing and Cooking with Herbs for our new book?"

He stopped harvesting some chives in mid-snip.

"You think a chapter on that will be good for your image?"

I frowned. "What do you mean?"

"Well, you two go around preaching about how much you love the plants and you talk to them and they're your friends. Won't people get mad if you start talking about eating them?"

I laughed. I knew Frenchy's tongue was buried in his cheek, but I couldn't resist a riposte.

"Not at all," I said. "Everybody knows that some plants—like Vegetables and Herbs—aren't born to be decorative, they're born to be eaten!"

Frenchy slowly grinned. "I like that," he said. "In fact, I think that's what I'll call my chapter!"

BORN TO BE EATEN
by
R. M. (Frenchy) DeLago

It's terrible, they did it again for the third time. Godzilla and her husband Chitty and the six catlets, true Russian Blue Bolsheviks they are, ruined four well-growing Herb pots hung high up in the air.

"I better go get them some Cat-Pot," said Loretta.

"No, Loretta, not Cat-Pot, as you insist on calling it. Catnip. It is a mintily fragrant Herb, it is not narcotic or habit-forming, but cats—all the cats, lions, tigers, pumas and alleycats are crazy about it and lose all self-respect and dignity as soon as they smell it. They eat it fresh or dried, roll in it, detect its presence from blocks away, and by the way if you want to get even with that gossipy woman down the street, get some and put it on her front lawn or better yet under her door mat. I assure you she will be extremely popular with all the felines for blocks who will persistently visit and loudly sing her praises for days to come."

"That's a good idea," said Loretta. "Where can I buy some of that Cat-Pot?"

"Not Cat-Pot, Catnip. My cats are not hopheads!"

So Loretta bought some Nepeta cataria (Catnip), and the next thing she was growing Herbs all over the place and so can you.

Here are some good Herbs and how to grow them and what to use them in:

Sweet Basil (Ocimum basilicum)—As the name itself will tell you, it is the King of Herbs (Gr. *Basilikos*—Royal). Basil has a strongly aromatic clove-like taste and is easy to grow from seed in window boxes, in pots, or outside in soil in early spring. It grows all year, but pinch back the flowers to prevent legginess. Likes full sun. You can use Basil with all seafood, most soups, salads, meat and poultry stews, liver, gravies, stuffings, venison and game, baked and broiled fish, and vegetables.

Since there are so many poor people in the world (the Lord loves them otherwise he wouldn't have created so many), they had to find ways to eat and eat well if possible, so they invented pasta. They took flour, water, an egg if they could find one, and made a lump of dough, flattened between two stones. They let it dry for a while and then cut it into different shaped pieces, making noodles, gnocchi, dumplings, lasagne, spaghetti, etc. So far, so good. But it tasted lousy. So they had to invent a sauce for it to make it edible and the cheapest one was pesto. Basil grew wild all around the Mediterranean Basin, and olives and pine-nuts were plentiful. Ergo, here is one of my favorite recipes using Basil.

One cup of fresh Basil, four cloves of garlic, one-fourth cup of parsley, one-third cup of olive oil (I mean OLIVE OIL), one-half cup of pignoli (pine-nuts or walnut meats), 2 tablespoons of water or consomme. Put the whole schmear into your blender and crush to a fine consistency. Cook your pasta al dente—not mushy—drain well—mix in some butter and grated parmesan cheese, mix in your pesto and buon appetito!

The Onion Family (Lilies)—"L'oignon est le roi des legumes" (The Onion is the king of vegetables), the French say. Truly the onion is indispensable to good, or even bad, cooking. Included in the family are the Spanish Onion, Bermuda, Red, White Pearl, Chive, Leek and Garlic. You can grow some Shallots and Chives from seed in rich soil on your kitchen window and then harvest by snipping off the leaves with a scissors to use raw in most of your cooked foods.

Here is a story that you might like, as well as a recipe for Zuppa Pavese (Italian Onion Soup) that you will definitely like.

In 1796, Napoleon Bonaparte occupied northern Italy and subjected the city of Pavia to a Three-Day Pillage as the city had revolted.

So when he got to Pavia there was very little left to eat. The farmer in whose house he and his General Staff stayed was ordered to whip up a meal—"And it better be damned good!"

"But Sire, your soldiers took all I had and left me only a few eggs, a bin of onions, some cheese, and a couple of hens and an old rooster. But I will do my best." And the farmer did.

So take lots of Onions, slice them fine, saute them in your soup-pot in butter, chicken fat, bacon fat, olive oil or whatever you have handy (do not brown the Onions, but cook them until they are soft and transparent). Remember the secret of Onion soup is Onions, Onions, and more Onions. I use for an Onion soup for 6 persons 10 to 12 pounds of Onions. Add 1 cup chicken stock, or consomme, or use a rooster as the farmer did if you can find one; boil the Onions and the stock slowly and season to taste with Bayleaf and 2 or 3 cloves of Garlic. Add salt and pepper, then put the soup in an ovenware pot, toast slices of French bread, put on top of the soup and sprinkle with grated Swiss cheese. It has to be Swiss because Swiss cheese is stringy. What you got now is a French Onion Soup.

Some people add some heavy cream to it and some dry white wine, but it's not important. For the Zuppa Pavese, proceed as with the French up to the bread. Then put the soup into oven-resistant pots, and on each individual pot put a good slice of Italian bread which has been abundantly sprinkled with freshly grated Parmesan cheese. Put in oven on high heat, and when your cheesed toast on top of the soup starts to bubble, crack one egg on top of the works and after about five more minutes serve as hot as you can. Eater beware, or you burn your beak.

Oregano—or wild Marjoram (Origanum vulgare). It is stronger than the Sweet Marjoram and is preferred by Latins and Mediterraneans. Grown easily in pots in your Herb garden. Just keep on the dry side. Use in stews, soup, tomato seasonings, gumbos, borsch, chowders, pork, veal, lamb, poultry, duck stuffings, most vegetables and omelettes. Indispensable in Italian pasta dishes.

Parsley (Petroselinum crispum)—Grows easily in pots on your kitchen window in mostly shade. Universally used with all meats and fish, vegetables, cheese and eggs.

Rosemary (Rosmarinus officinalis)—Unique, spicy, pungent odor and flavor. Difficult to grow but easy to buy. Propagated from cutting in spring as seeds are hard to come by. Plant in full sun in light soil. Add lime to the soil to help growth and keep on the dry side. Used in soups and chowders, green vegetables, meat, poultry, game stuffings, fish, eggplants, turnips, etc.

Sage (Salvia officinalis)—This strongly accented flavorful and pungent Herb will grow readily in pots if kept dry, well drained, and in a warm, sunny location. Sage belongs to the mint family, and can also be propagated from cuttings. USE SPARINGLY in soups, meats, fowl, fish, vegetables. Sage can also be used as a decorative plant, as the Scarlet Sage.

Mint—Mint grows wild in most of the United States and prefers damp places in shade or in hanging pots. It's used for many things, but mainly Mint Juleps or as a sauce for lamb.

If you want the recipe for a Mint Julep, ask any respectable bartender, because I forget it after three good ones.

So now that we had a Mint Julep or two, let's make Roast Leg of Lamb Boulangère (Baker's style) with Mint Sauce.

You may notice I didn't mention a meat dish yet, because Mother and Father Earth don't like meat so much. They prefer vegetables and occasionally chicken or fish, but I say baloney and I mean the meat. Homo sapiens is omnivorous; he eats anything. I, in my travels, have eaten kangaroo tails in Australia, grasshoppers in Abyssinia, honeyed termites in Somaliland, and tapir steaks in South Africa. I am 75 years old, feel fine, and laugh down the graves of my cholesterol-starved friends.

Now since I got the venom out of my soul, let's get on with the brisket of lamb. Use about a 4-pound piece of brisket. Like everything else, you get what you pay for. There's lamb and there's lamb. You will have to pay for a real good leg of lamb—maybe as much as $15—but you can get a very promising looking leg for about $4. Don't be fooled. The $15 leg is tender, cooks faster, is not stringy or tough or goaty as your Gorilla Leg for $4. So take your good leg of lamb and ask the butcher to bone it and tie it for you. That's the way I do it. Then I prepare a mixture of Herbs: chopped Garlic, Basil, Marjoram, Rosemary, salt, pepper, Sage, and any other of the Capitol sins you might fancy. Oh, don't forget the chopped pine-nuts or walnuts and a few leaves of Mint, and tell the butcher to put it in the center of the boned and rolled-tied lamb leg. Save the bones for a good barley-lamb soup. Wrap your doctored-up leg in foil and put in the refrigerator, not freezer, for two to six days. The Herbs in the leg will permeate the meat and marinate it. Now on the day of your dinner, put your leg on a rotisserie or on a rack in the oven at the highest possible heat for 10 minutes to sear and seal in your juices. Then reduce your heat to 300 degrees and insert a meat thermometer in the thickest part of the meat. When the thermometer reaches 150 degrees, remove the roast, let it stand, and it will continue to cook in its own heat. To cook your lamb will take about one and a half hours for rare. I myself like it pink rather than well done, although many expensive and excellent meat cuts have been loused up by food-faddists.

Serve your lamb with potatoes and onions with Rosemary leaves and, of course, either Mint jelly you make yourself which is a big pain or the commercial Mint jelly which is easier.

Tarragon (Artemisia dracunculus)—Its unusual, intriguing anise-like (licorice) flavor is vigorously fragrant and widely used in gourmet cooking. Hard to grow from seed, needing rich, well-drained soil and partial shade, it's used in sauces, salads, fish, meats, vegetables, cheese, and eggs, and to flavor vinegar.

Thyme (Thymus vulgaris)—grows wild in the Mediterranean Basin. It is easy to grow in a light, dry soil and full sun. There are a number of varieties and each has a little different flavor. It is used fresh or dried, in soups, seafood, chicken, meat, and all vegetables.

There is an old saying about food that I made up many years ago: If something tastes good alone, why shouldn't it taste good with something else that tastes good? The same is true of Herbs. You can mix several Herbs together in several different ways and wind up with unique and excellent taste treats. Some Herb mixtures that I like to use are

1. Herb Butters—Combine Herbs with fats, unsalted butter, margarine, pork drippings, chicken fat, etc. Use 2 full tablespoons of fresh Herbs or 2 teaspoons of dried Herbs to a 4-ounce stick of butter. Let your chopped Herbs stand for a few minutes in some fresh lemon juice before blending with butter or fat. Store in refrigerator and use cold on sandwiches and pour melted on steaks, chops, etc.

Best Herbs for this use are Parsley, Chives, Tarragon and Marjoram.

2. Fines Herbes—A combination of Herbs such as Basil, Marjoram, Rosemary, Tarragon, Thyme and Chives, finely chopped and sieved and added directly to most of your salads, soups, meats, vegetables, etc.

3. Bouquet Garni—A selection of fresh or dried Herbs such as Basil, Savory, Marjoram, Thyme, Onion, Bay leaf, Celery leaf, all tied in a small cheesecloth bag and immersed into such foods as soups, sauces, stews, and removed before serving.

For good results in cooking with Herbs, please use the following general rules:

- Don't overuse. Too much obliterates the taste of your cooking. It is better too little than too much.
- Chop or cut your fresh Herbs very fine or better yet crush in mortar.
- Remember, dried Herbs are three or four times stronger than fresh Herbs, so use less dried than fresh. Buy only small quantities of Herbs, as they lose their strength, flavor, and aroma over a short time.
- The aroma and flavor of your Herbs are lost by overcooking.

Oh, oh. Chitty is trying to be a father again and Godzilla don't like it and she isn't ready yet, so I have to go now. Bon appétit, and I hope I see you next time.

THE END

Please follow these rules.

Toaay's sermon: How Plants Can Change Your Life.

As we indicated in the Foreword and have kept implying throughout the book, what we're really trying to do this time around is to help you understand what your plants can do for *you*, to give you some hints on how to find more joys from your Green Experience than you can think up by yourself. Most of the suggestions have come from other plant freaks we've talked with, not from us (although we do have a couple of little tips out of our own experience).

We've already established that the Plant Fever is sweeping the land, that it extends far beyond the mere use of houseplants as home decor. Besides the plants themselves that are becoming so evident in virtually every store or office we frequent, plant "things" are also beginning to sprout: plant sheets, plant wallpaper, plant fabrics, plant print, plant everything!

So let the Fever rage on, say the Plant People and the Plant Doctors alike, we among both groups. It's an easy disease to diagnose, this Plant Fever. People afflicted get a Rosy glow (not a green pallor as you might suspect), a feeling of inner peace instead of a queasy stomach, and when they talk of their addiction—"I swear, I've got a Begonia on my back!"—they sound as if they're involved in a truly spiritual experience—a religion, in fact!

Plantology!

Why not?

No sense beating around the Bonsai. As Missionaries of the Green, we're here to proselytize, to try to convert you to Plantology. This doesn't mean we suggest you give up your God for a Dracaena. Plantology is compatible with any religion under the sun (a few hours a day, at any rate).

Why do our little green friends stir up these such enormous emotions? There are lots of reasons, we suppose, but the one single answer—the mystique, as it were—is beyond our comprehension and we simply accept it and know in our hearts that it's right.

Blind Faith, we guess it's called.

We've gotten letters from all over the country from people assuring us their conversion to Plantology has changed their lives—in some instances, even saved them. (As they say in the commercials, "Documentation of these

131

statements available upon request at the Little Church of the Spathiphyllum.")

So because we want you to become *totally* involved, not just to the point of having plants in your home but of making them part of your entire life, we will preach you a sermon. To her own Jack-in-the-Pulpit now comes the High Priestess of Plantology, The Green Reverend Ms. Mother Earth.

Welcome, Brothers and Sisters!

Today's sermon is entitled "How Plants Can Change Your Life," which regular members of the congregation know is the title of every day's sermon. Before I begin, let me be sure you have all knelt at the Shrine of the African Violet (our beloved patron Saintpaulia) and examined her for mealybug or other signs of the Devil himself.

Hallelujah!

Let us begin. In the Age of the Plant, it is no longer necessary nor warranted to confine your use of indoor plants to home decor. In fact, my friends, it is plain ridiculous! What about your office, or your place of business? Every place benefits from the use of plants. Any place can be beautified and made more natural in feeling by the addition of just a few healthy, lush, tropical greens. Why, my friends, must some of you still cling to your plastic rubber trees when real rubber trees would thrive just as well, if not better?

I smile, my friends, when I think of a certain dentist among us, a recent convert, who shamedly told me in the confessional last week that it had taken him almost three years to get rid of the plastic plants in his waiting room and replace them with the real McCoy. In his own words, getting him to make the switch was like pulling teeth. But already, Brothers and Sisters, he admits his patients are more relaxed when they sit down in his chair, and some don't even need anesthetic anymore! We say to you, Doctor—that's a Gas, and we assure you when Gabriel blows his Trumpet Vine, yours shall be the Goldest filling of them all! Hallelujah!

Brothers and Sisters, I say unto you: Plastic plants are offensive! If you are serious in your role as members of the Church of Plantology, if you wish to don the Bishop's Hat,

Plant Fever is sweeping the land.

A bank's main commodity is green stuff.

then let it be known that plastic plants are false gods and those who cling to their worship are just not hip to what's happening! Dare you speak your feelings to these heathens without fear of being considered a fanatic, or rude? That's up to you, my friends—but I say that if you Believe, to keep silent is a greater sin against the Mother Fern! So speak out, safe in the knowledge that what you do is Right!

Do I hear a whisper of disbelief? Then hark to the story of a banker who replaced his plastic plants with live ones when a fervent group of Plantologists threatened to take their accounts elsewhere unless he put live plants in his branch, and live leaves on his branches! He complied, my friends, and admitted later than since the addition of the real plants, his business like his plants has grown. He was surprised, but we weren't. After all, hasn't a bank's main commodity always been green stuff?

Are you beginning to see the light, Brothers and Sisters? Indirect, that is, or even fluorescent.

Hallelujah!

Hark! Do I feel the thoughts of a first-time visitor? I'm getting a message ... "What if there isn't enough light to grow anything in my place?" To you, I say, if you live or work in a place that's too dark for live plants—no windows, no fluorescent lighting—then I say to you it's too dark for live people and my advice is to move out before you turn into a Mushroom!

Amen, amen!

My friends, there is a story I must tell you that will show you why I believe in miracles.

It is a story of how a fellow Plantologist saved his restaurant from bankruptcy by the ingenious use of plants and far-out containers. I suppose you wonder why I would speak to you of decorating a restaurant when 52 percent of you don't own restaurants, 36 percent can't afford to eat out, and 13 percent are undecided.

Because, Brothers and Sisters, I want you to feel the joy I felt when I saw a person born anew because of plants!

Hallelujah!

He came to me, smelling of garlic and lemon and all the wondrous odors of our brothers, the Herbs and Spices, and looked into my eyes. "Ms. Mother," he said, "I have had a vision and it has brought me into your Temple of the Ti Plant! I own a restaurant as you may have smelled. The food I cook is overwhelming. But my bank account is overdrawn. I was at my wit's end as to how to avoid bankruptcy, and then last night there came a vision. I saw, as big as life and just as green, Dancing Dieffenbachias, Spinning Spider Plants, Frolicking Ferns—and I then knew the Answer. Please, Ms. Mother, come put plants in my restaurant and make it beautiful so people will flock to taste of my moderately priced cuisine. Diners Club and American Express accepted—No checks please."

I looked at him and said, "My son, there is no doubt you have found the Answer in plant decor. But it must be as a result of your own love and labor. Take a copy of our Bible—our regular members will know I handed him not a copy of the New or Old Testament, but the Green Testament—*Mother Earth's Hassle-Free Indoor Plant Book*—and I said unto him, "Use this, and your imagination and your days of sadness will turn to days of joy. Remember, your restaurant is an empty canvas, you are the artist, and plants are your paints. Go, my son, and believe that when you have done, your bank account will walk again."

One month later I was invited to his restaurant for lunch. Friends, I had to wait twenty minutes for a table! Yes, you heard me, Brothers and Sisters, twenty minutes! But those twenty minutes were some of the happiest of my life. Why, my friends? Because I was surrounded by plants! A Kentia Palm in the corner, small live plants as centerpieces on every table, all planted in antique cookware and old teapots and creamers. Other kitchen objects—copper pots, urns, utensils—were filled with the hardiest of plants and placed most creatively on shelves all about the room. The owner—and I say this with the most humble pride, my friends—kissed my ring, a tiny Bromeliad tied to a small loop around my finger—and, my friends, he looked at me with a tear in his eye.

"Thank you, Ms. Mother," he said. "And Praise be to them!" He pointed to the myriad of plants in the room. "They are so beautiful, I love them all. And look at those Ferns and Spider Plants I hung up. I made sure they didn't

If it's too dark for live plants,
it's too dark for live people.

Give plants.

dangle in the diners' dinners!"

Oh, my friends, he was so proud of what he had created, and I knew as I looked at him that the Garden Path I have chosen to tread is worth treading no matter what may leap up to block my way—Red Spider, Scale, Mealybug—none of these things shall ever turn me away from my chosen destiny! I shall never remove this Rosary Plant from around my neck. And I shall kneel to my Prayer Plant and ask that you, too, follow the same course!

Amen! Hallelujah! Right on!

It won't all be a bed of Roses, my friends. I have suffered many slings and arrows, for instance, for my penchant of the wearing of plants. My Bromeliad ring has been chided as bizarre; my hat which holds a 2-inch Philodendron in its brim has been laughed at. You heard me, my friends, a plant has been laughed at, may Saint-paulia have mercy on their souls. That I carry a bag full of plants wherever I go has been looked upon askance, but to all who would mock me I answer, fie on you! Plants are my friends and I must have them with me wherever I go!

Amen!

It's odd, my friends, that some of the same people who would have the men in the Green Coats come to put me forthwith into the nearest padded pot are the same people who don't notice that if someone brings a plant into the office for their desk, others will soon start to pop up on other desks—without propagation! Could you dare to be a perpetrator of this Immaculate Conception in your office? I say to you it is your duty, my friends, just as surely as it's your duty not to be a litterbug!

Carry with you always the tenets of Plantology: Instead of liquor or wine, give plants when you go to someone's house for dinner. At Halloween give out plants instead of candy. Don't be afraid to pick a yellow leaf from a plant wherever you see it. Give plants as party favors at children's birthdays. Never buy a plant unless you know it's healthy, and never buy a plant unless you know for sure it will thrive in the conditions in which you intend to put it. Believe in the rightness of what you're doing, Brothers and Sisters, and remember, there are no atheists in a Greenhouse!

Before we conclude our services with a hymn from *Psalms to the Palms*—page 43, "Praise be to Thee, Oh Angel-Wing Begonia"—I beg you, my friends, get out there and recruit *your* friends for our next session and always remember the basic Commandments of Plantology: Thou shalt not overwater, thou shalt not overfeed, thou shalt not talk harshly to thy plants, but it's okay to covet your neighbor's cuttings.

Amen, Brothers and Sisters—and Happy Growing!

Wasn't that a great sermon Ms. Mother Earth just preached? And best of all (if you were paying attention) did you notice she didn't pass a collection plate at the end?

Hallelujah! ⟋⟍

Index Continued